To- David
From- Gwenda
2023

THE
ORDNANCE SURVEY
PUZZLE BOOK
LEGENDS AND
LANDMARKS

THE ORDNANCE SURVEY PUZZLE BOOK LEGENDS AND LANDMARKS

Can **YOU** solve over 250
clues on an adventure
through Britain's heroic history

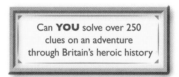
Ordnance
Survey

By Ordnance Survey, Daniel Peake and
Emma Russell

SEVEN DIALS

Mapping images © Crown Copyright and database rights 2023
Text and other images © Ordnance Survey Limited 2023
Puzzles © The Orion Publishing Group Ltd 2021
Puzzles by Daniel Peake

The right of the Ordnance Survey to be identified as
the authors of this work has been asserted in accordance with the
Copyright, Designs and Patents Act 1988.

This edition first published in Great Britain in 2023 by Seven Dials
an imprint of the Orion Publishing Group Ltd
Carmelite House
50 Victoria Embankment
London EC4Y 0DZ

An Hachette UK Company

1 3 5 7 9 10 8 6 4 2

ISBN: 978 1 3996 1107 7

Printed in Italy

MIX
Paper from
responsible sources
FSC® C104740

www.orionbooks.co.uk

CONTENTS

Foreword....................................6

Introduction..............................8

Map Reading Fundamentals................ 10

Common Map Abbreviations and Symbols...14

An Introduction to the Puzzles 16

PUZZLES

Kingdom Shapers 18

Political Challengers.......................48

How to Spot History on a Map..............70

Health and Social Reformers...............74

Science Makers 96

Iconic Film and TV Locations 122

Artistic Creators.........................126

Shakers and Movers 160

Recommended Things To Do.............182

Solutions................................187

Your Notes...............................224

Ordnance Survey Map Information 234

Ordnance Survey Sheet Index............ 236

Credits 238

Acknowledgements 239

FOREWORD

Much of my life has been spent on athletics tracks, and my career as a sprinter has given me the opportunity to travel the globe making some amazing memories. As a young boy, I never dreamt that one day I would become the British 400m record holder, a European, Commonwealth and World champion.

Although I made a career from sport, the love of being outside and on the move has always been a part of me. I was one of those kids who would run everywhere: to my mate's house, to the shops, to school. I loved running, being outdoors. It made me feel alive, exhilarated and free. It was a joy of life, unencumbered by self-consciousness or worries. I just wanted to get out. I had energy to spare and still have to this day. If I can't work out every day, I feel restless and agitated. I believe sport and exercise have something positive to offer everyone. When I go running or get a session in at the gym, that is my way of switching off and escaping. Life throws many challenges at us, and we deal with stress in different ways, but for me exercise is my happy place – it always has been. With a busy balance between work and family, exercise can be the one thing that drops down your to-do list. When life gets stressful I know where to turn, to that trusted friend, the one thing that can switch my mood, a constant for as long as I can remember: sport.

Throughout my sprinting career, I did suffer from injuries at times. When I was unable to train or compete, it really affected me, not only physically but also psychologically. However, once I was able to get back to training, my sense of wellbeing improved.

I now call the southeast of England home, with my family. On my doorstep I have the New Forest and South Downs National Park, and The Solent, with views over to the Isle of Wight. There are plenty of places for me to get out and enjoy the fresh air with the family or by myself and admire the beautiful scenery and wildlife. This can be extremely calming, being at one with nature. Sport and exercise does not have to be adrenaline-filled and pushing your body hard. Exercise can be as simple as a gentle walk with your dog or exploring somewhere new on an easy bike ride with a friend. The benefits are massive for your mental health by getting outside either by yourself or with friends and family.

Running is still a massive part of my life; I have completed the London Marathon eight times, and completed my first ever 100-mile ultramarathon along the South Downs Way in 2021. My personal values align so much with Ordnance Survey's mission to help more people get outside more often, and understanding a place, knowing where to go and making sure you have the most up-to-date mapping to help keep you safe is super important. OS products enable you to do this, exploring with confidence and creating the best memories in the outdoors. I want to be remembered for my service to athletics and charity, and in this book you will explore many of Great Britain's Legends and Landmarks. Hopefully this inspires you to get outside and give yourself some 'you' time. Go find your happy place.

Iwan Thomas, MBE

INTRODUCTION

Great Britain has such a varied landscape, from the beautiful sandy beaches of Cornwall in the southwest to the heights of the Cairngorm Plateau in the northeast of Scotland. Many legends call Great Britain home, either by being born here or choosing to live their lives here. All of those featured in this book have contributed to society, to help shape and form the world we live in today.

Ordnance Survey has its roots in military strategy, and one legend who mapped the Scottish Highlands following the Jacobite Rebellion in 1745 was William Roy, a young engineer at just twenty-one. He went on to create what was known as The Great Map, which took him eight years to complete. The map included recordings of roads, hills, rivers and settlements. William's contribution remains at the heart of Ordnance Survey.

We have picked a selection of legends from across Great Britain and explored the places that moulded them. It was very hard to pick, there are so many inspiring people who called Great Britain home at one point in their life. We hope this book will spark your imagination and inspire you to find out more about both them and the landmarks and landscapes that sculpted them.

There are many places to explore and discover in Great Britain; some might be unfamiliar, and some might be closer to home. At Ordnance Survey we are obsessed by the wonders of the outdoors. We strive every day to help more people get outside more often and enjoy the outdoors, from a single day trip to planning an epic journey. For me, there remains a certain sense of wonderment that comes from taking a map off the bookshelf, unfurling it, and letting my adventurous side take over as I explore the creases and contours of the land. Despite digital technology, I can still lose myself in a map, tucked up in the living room looking at OS Maps online, plotting a new route, searching for my next adventure.

The Covid-19 pandemic showed us all how important it is to look after our mental health, especially as so many of us spent lockdown looking at the same four walls of our living room. Medical professionals even recommend spending more time outside in the fresh air, engaging with and exploring the landscape, as this has such a massive benefit to our mental and physical health. Better still, the outdoors is free for everyone to use and enjoy. This makes our mission to inspire more people to get outside more often even more important in today's world. The outdoors has something to offer everyone, and it does not have to be a strenuous ascent or summitting a challenging mountain.

From exploring our varied history and visiting our older cities such as Edinburgh, York or London, all of which are steeped in history, to searching for film and TV locations, as the landscape and architecture of Great Britain is being used increasingly for filming. There are some iconic sights to discover, such as Glenfinnan Viaduct and Alnwick Castle (Harry Potter franchise), Rosslyn Chapel on the outskirts of Edinburgh (*The Da Vinci Code*) or Levisham in the North York Moors (Mission: Impossible franchise). Great Britain has so much to offer!

We hope that by completing these puzzles you are inspired to get outside and plan your next adventure, be that close to home or further afield. If you need more information, guidance or inspiration, then visit getoutside.uk.

Happy exploring!

Nick Giles OBE

Managing Director – Ordnance Survey Leisure

PS We would love to hear your suggestions on our social media pages, #OSPuzzletime.
Find us on Twitter @OSleisure, Instagram @ordnancesurvey and Facebook @osmapping.

TO HELP YOU EXPLORE GREAT BRITAIN USING ORDNANCE SURVEY MAPS, WE HAVE CREATED SOME MAP READING FUNDAMENTALS.

WHAT IS A MAP?

A map is simply a drawing or picture of a landscape or location. Maps usually show the landscape as it would be seen from above, looking directly down. As well as showing the landscape of an area, maps will often show other features such as roads, rivers, buildings, trees and lakes.

A map can allow you to accurately plan a journey, giving a good idea of landmarks and features you will pass along the route, as well as how far you will be travelling.

MAP SYMBOLS

Understanding map symbols is key to understanding what's on a map. Symbols are used to show where certain things are, so that maps don't have to be covered in writing. Ordnance Survey uses different shapes, colours and symbols to show the roads, buildings, rivers and other features of a landscape. Symbols are designed to be simple; you can explore Ordnance Survey's Common Map Abbreviations and Symbols on the previous page.

MAP SCALE

To create an accurate picture of a landscape on paper, everything has to be made much, much smaller. This is done by scaling down the actual size of the land.

This also means we have to simplify and remove features. Thick hedges, stone walls and fences are all shown as thin black lines on Explorer maps and not at all on Landranger. Roads are exaggerated so that they are wide enough to fill with colour. Buildings are merged together and garden sheds ignored.

Ordnance Survey have two main map series for exploring Great Britain: Explorer, printed at a scale of 1:25 000, and Landranger, printed at a scale of 1:50 000. Explorer has the most detail, ideal for walking. Landranger maps have slightly less detail but cover a wider area, ideal for biking or a multi-day trip. Each scale includes the National Grid as thin blue lines, spaced one kilometre apart.

To help you solve the puzzles in this book, we have enlarged the Explorer and Landranger maps to 1:20 000 and 1:40 000 respectively. The following examples show the same area at the two scales of mapping:(1:50 000) below:

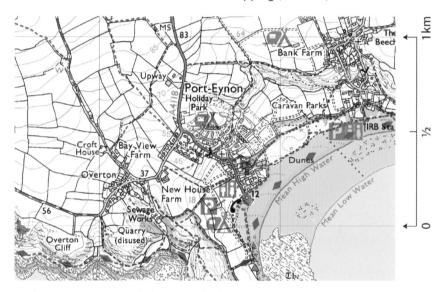

Explorer at 1:20 000 scale (5cm to 1 km)

Landranger at 1:40 000 scale
(2.5 cm to 1 km)

GRID REFERENCES

Ordnance Survey maps are covered in a series of faint blue lines that make up a grid. The lines have numbers accompanying them that allow you to accurately pinpoint your location on a map.

Before you begin to look at grid references it is important to be aware that all the numbers going across the face of the map, for example, left to right, are called eastings (this is because they are heading eastward), and similarly, all the numbers going up the face of the map, from bottom to top, are called northings (because they are heading in a northward direction).

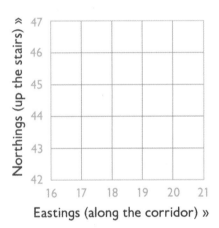

There are two main types of grid reference:

- 4-figure – for example 1945, which identifies a single kilometre square on an OS map.

- 6-figure – for example 192454, which identifies a 100-metre square within a single kilometre square on an OS map.

The grid reference is always for the bottom left-hand corner of the grid square you are in.

To understand how to do 4-figure and 6-figure grid references, please refer to our more detailed Ordnance Survey Map Reading Guides (see QR codes below).

READING CONTOURS AND RELIEF

The height and shape of the land is shown on a map using 'contour lines'. These lines appear as thin orange or brown lines with numbers on them. The number tells you the height above sea level of that line. A contour line is drawn between points of equal height, so any single contour line will be at the same height all the way along its length. The height difference between separate contour lines is normally 10 metres, but it will be 5 metres in flatter areas.

Please scan the QR codes below to take you to our Map Reading Guides.

Map Reading Made Easy:

Map Reading: From the beginner to the advanced map reader:

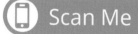

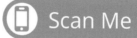

COMMON MAP ABBREVIATIONS AND SYMBOLS

SELECTED TOURIST AND LEISURE SYMBOLS

The style, size and colour of these symbols vary across map series, or may be described by text with no symbol.

🏛	Art gallery (notable / important)	Ⓜ	Museum
	Boat hire		National Trust
	Boat trips		Nature reserve
	Building of historic interest	☆	Other tourist feature
	Cadw (Welsh Heritage)	P	Parking
⋏	Camp site	P&R	Park and ride, all year
	Camping and caravan site	P&R	Park and ride, seasonal
	Caravan site		Phone; public, emergency
	Castle or fort	✕	Picnic site
✝	Cathedral or abbey		Preserved railway
	Country park		Public house(s)
	Craft centre		Public toilets
	Cycle hire	Ⓧ	Recreation, leisure or sports centre
	Cycle trail		Slipway
	English Heritage		Theme or pleasure park
	Fishing		Viewpoint
	Garden or arboretum	V	Visitor centre
⌐	Golf course or links	❗	Walks or trails
HC	Heritage centre		Water activities (board)
	Historic Scotland		Water activities (paddle)
U	Horse riding		Water activities (powered)
𝒊	Information centre		Water activities (sailing)
𝒊	Information centre, seasonal		Watersports centre (multi-activity)
	Mountain bike trail	⊚	World Heritage site / area

ABBREVIATIONS

Acad	Academy	Ind Est	Industrial Estate	Rd	Road		
BP	Boundary Post	La	Lane	Rems	Remains		
BS	Boundary Stone	LC	Level Crossing	Resr	Reservoir		
CG	Cattle Grid	Liby	Library	Rly	Railway		
CH	Clubhouse	Mkt	Market	Sch	School		
Cotts	Cottages	Meml	Memorial	St	Saint / Street		
Dis	Disused	MP	Milepost	Twr	Tower		
Dismtd	Dismantled	MS	Milestone	TH	Town Hall		
Fm	Farm	Mon	Monument	Uni	University		
F Sta	Fire Station	PH	Public House	NTL	Normal Tidal Limit		
FB	Footbridge	P, PO	Post Office	Wks	Works		
Ho	House	Pol Sta	Police station	°W; Spr	Well; Spring		

PUBLIC RIGHTS OF WAY

OS Landranger	OS Explorer		
·················	▪▪▪▪▪▪▪▪▪▪▪	Footpath	**The representation on the maps of any**
― ― ― ― ― ― ―	▬ ▬ ▬ ▬ ▬	Bridleway	**other road, track or path is no evidence**
-+-+-+-+-+-+	┿ ┿ ┿ ┿ ┿	Byway open to all traffic	**of the existence of a right of way.**
-·-·-·-·-·-·-	┷ ┷ ┷ ┷ ┷	Restricted byway (not for use by mechanically propelled vehicles)	

The symbols show the defined route so far as the scale of mapping will allow. Rights of way are liable to change and may not be clearly defined on the ground. Please check with the relevant local authority for the latest information. Rights of way are not shown on maps of Scotland, where rights of responsible access apply.

PUBLIC ACCESS

OS Landranger	OS Explorer	
◆ ◆ ◆	◆ ◆ ◆	National Trail , Scotland's Great Trails European Long Distance Route and selected recreational routes
• • • • •	n/a	Other route with public access (not normally shown in urban areas)

 Danger Area

Firing and test ranges in the area. Danger!
Observe warning notices
Visit: **gov.uk/guidance/public-access-to-military-areas**

ACCESS LAND

Access land (symbols indicate owner or agency – see below)

🟢	Forestry England	🟢🟢		National Trust; always open, limited access – observe local signs
⊗	Natural Resources Wales	🟥		Woodland Trust Land
🟢	Forestry and Land Scotland	🟦🟦		National Trust for Scotland; always open, limited access – observe local signs

Access land portrayed on Explorer maps is intended as a guide to land normally available for access on foot, for example access land created under the Countryside and Rights of Way Act 2000, and land managed by National Trust, Forestry Commission, Woodland Trust and Natural Resources Wales. Some restrictions will apply; some land shown as access land may not have open access rights; always refer to local signage.

ARCHAEOLOGICAL AND HISTORICAL INFORMATION

⚔ 1066	Site of battle (with date)	VILLA	Roman	Information sourced from Historic England, Historic
☆ ▥▥▥	Visible earthwork	𝕮astle	Non-Roman	Environment Scotland and the Royal Commission on the Ancient and Historical Monuments of Wales.

LAND FEATURES

⊞⊞ ⊞⊞	Cutting, embankment	⩘ Beacon ⊤ Mast	
⬭	Bus or coach station	⌖ Lighthouse	
⬙	Glasshouse or structure	⌖ Lighthouse; disused	
△	Triangulation pillar	⌇ Wind pump	
+	Place of worship	⊥ Wind turbine	
Current or former place of worship;		⋇ Windmill (with or without sails)	
⏁	with tower	▨ Solar Farm	
⏁	with spire, minaret or dome		

BOUNDARIES

OS Landranger	OS Explorer
National	
┿ ▬ ┿ ▬	┿ ― ┿ ―
County	
▬·▬·▬·▬·	― · ― · ―
Unitary Authority or London Borough	
▬·▬·▬·▬·	
District	
┿ · ┿ · ┿ ·	― ― ―

AN INTRODUCTION TO THE PUZZLES

You are about to embark on a puzzle tour of Great Britain and meet some of the people who have lived here over the centuries. The inhabitants of this ancient land have woven its identity, they've created a tapestry of stories and shaped the cultural fabric of the nation. 'Legends and Landmarks' is a celebration of the people who have accomplished extraordinary things, and through their determination, we have benefitted from their skills, talent and bravery.

There are plenty of puzzles along the way; a mix of word puzzles, search-and-find clues, general knowledge questions, and navigation trails to follow. These conundrums will test the skills of map readers of every level. You will also find snippets of information, places of interest, and some ideas for future outings and real-life adventures of your own.

Great Britain is an island of vast geographical variety, from forests and farms to streets and cities, there is so much to explore. Ordnance Survey maps have evolved to reflect this ever-changing country, to mark new roads and byways, footpaths and boundaries. We can easily identify physical features on a map, the natural curves of rolling hills and bends in rivers, or the sharp edges of man-made museums and churches. It's not so easy to see the people who have lived here. Steeped in a rich heritage that spans time, Britain is a land where history and myth intertwine and tales of valiant heroes have been passed down through the generations. Every step resonates with the echoes of a historic past.

Some of these individuals are world-famous and most are well-known, but there may be a few that you've never heard of and we are delighted to have brought their personal narratives to your attention. We hope you enjoy the journey!

Important to note: heights are in metres above mean sea level and are shown by black numbers or orange numbers on the map. Black heights have been surveyed on the ground and orange from the air. The vertical height between contour lines on Explorer maps is 5 metres except for mountainous areas where they are 10 metres. You can use the contour values to check the interval. Landranger maps always have a 10 metre vertical distance.

David Stirling and
the Bridge of Allan

William Wallace
and Elderslie

Horatio Nelson and
Burnham Thorpe

Owain Glyndwr
and Sycharth

Alfred the Great and Wantage

Walter Raleigh
and Hayes Barton

Isambard Kingdom
Brunel and Portsmouth

KINGDOM
SHAPERS

1. *Alfred the Great*

———

2. *William Wallace*

———

3. *Owain Glyndwr*

———

4. *Walter Raleigh*

———

5. *Horatio Nelson*

———

6. *Isambard Kingdom Brunel*

———

7. *David Stirling*

Map 1 ALFRED THE GREAT AND WANTAGE

Alfred the Great was the King of Wessex, a kingdom that covered the south of Anglo-Saxon England. He is widely considered one of the most important monarchs in English history, strategically defending his kingdom against Viking invasion.

Alfred was born in Wantage in 849, and as the youngest son of King Æthelwulf, he was never expected to become king. However, he ascended the throne in 871 at the age of twenty-two, after the death of his older brother Æthelred, but the Vikings were an imminent threat, having overwhelmed most of England north of the River Thames.

Alfred won a decisive victory at the Battle of Edington in Wiltshire in 878. After the battle, he negotiated a peace treaty with Guthrum of the Vikings. This established a clear boundary between 'Danelaw', the Viking area, and the realm of England. The Treaty of Alfred and Guthrum was not formalised until 886, but it made provision for a peaceful co-existence between the English and the Vikings.

Alfred fortified towns along the border and reorganised his military to strengthen his defence against future attacks. He has been credited with the formation of the English Navy, building a fleet of fighting ships to combat Viking raids.

As a child, Alfred had travelled to Rome, and he was an educated man and a patron of learning who sponsored the translation of Latin works into Old English. He provided a translated version of the *Anglo-Saxon Chronicle*, a collection of written records that tell the story of the Anglo-Saxons in their own language. This promoted education and literacy amongst his people, which earned him the title 'Alfred the Great'. By initiating a series of legal and administrative reforms, Alfred was instrumental in codifying the laws within his own kingdom.

Around 886, Alfred referred to himself as King of the Anglo-Saxons and was established as the first in the unbroken line of kings of the House of Wessex. He died in 899 but his legacy continued to influence English history and culture. Known for his wisdom, piety and strong governance, he represents an important chapter in English history. He was succeeded by his son, Edward the Elder.

A statue in Wantage commemorates the birthplace of King Alfred the Great. It was sculpted in marble by Count Gleichen, Prince of Hohenlohe-Langenburg, and unveiled in 1877. Alfred holds a battleaxe in one hand and a manuscript in the other.

▪ Easy

1. How many springs are labelled with 'Spr' on the map?

2. Which location on the map has a name that rhymes with itself?

▪ Medium

3. Where might two winners of the 1966 FIFA World Cup feel at home?

4. Which of these is at a higher altitude: the crossing that gives the value of a long-time portrayer of M in Bond movies; or the building with this shape?

▪ Tricky

5. Find the 85m contour that passes through the label for the Grove Technology Park. How many letters (but not numbers) does this contour pass through in total on the map?

6. How many two-word labels on the map have the same number of letters in both words?

▪ Challenging

7. Start at the Academy surrounded by a 95m contour. Head west on the main road until it is 88m in altitude, then turn north. Continue until you reach a roundabout, then turn right. Turn left at the next roundabout. Take the exit off the A-road where you cross the path of a former waterway. Head north until you reach a school, then turn left. Go in that direction for approximately 720m until you reach a turn in the road. What number is traced out with this route?

8. Which places on the map are the answers to the following cryptic clues?

   – Rod's returned to relax around rising ground

   – Bobby's map has 'length' on

   – Nick tore load asunder in thoroughfare

   – Look through array at shooting gallery

Map 2 WILLIAM WALLACE AND ELDERSLIE

William Wallace was born sometime around 1270, in Elderslie, Renfrewshire. By the time he was in his twenties, Wallace was devoted to freeing Scotland from the tyranny of English rule. He killed the Sheriff of Lanark and led a band of outlaws, and their numbers grew until they formed an army. When Wallace joined forces with Andrew Moray, the rebellion became a revolution.

In 1297, Wallace and Moray fought the English at Stirling Bridge. Wallace did not adhere to the etiquette of war, and he outmanoeuvred the English, killing five thousand and claiming victory against all odds. Moray died from his wounds, but Wallace rose to prominence and defended the Borders.

Wallace was merciless and killed the English wherever he found them. Chronicles from that period in time are full of accounts of his unwavering savagery. After his campaign of terror, he was knighted by Scottish Lords and made Guardian of Scotland.

In 1298, Wallace was defeated by Edward I in the Battle of Falkirk where two thousand Scots died. He escaped with his life, but his reputation was in tatters. He was demoted from Guardian and retreated to Selkirk.

Wallace continued to fight for several more years, but he was betrayed by one of his servants. On 23 August 1305, Wallace was dragged through the streets of London, then hung, drawn and quartered, and his head displayed on London Bridge. His brutal execution inspired Robert the Bruce, who led the decisive Battle of Bannockburn in 1314. Bruce's victory changed Scotland

and established the freedom that Wallace had fought for. Wallace's tenacity and unwavering belief became his legacy.

In Elderslie, the Wallace Birthplace Monument was erected on the site of his home. Recent archaeological digs found evidence of the original building's foundations. The modern structure is in the shape of a market cross, with a series of sculpted plaques depicting the life of Wallace as Knight of Elderslie and Guardian of Scotland.

There are numerous tributes to Wallace across Scotland, including a song written by Robert Burns, 'Scots Wha Hae', which has become a nationalist anthem. Over seven hundred years after his death, Wallace continues to represent the pride and passion of the Scottish people.

■ Easy

1. Which building has this shape on the map?

2. Where might you have one hundred arguments?

■ Medium

3. Which way does Old Patrick Water run, northwards or southwards?

4. What is Dwayne Johnson adorned with?

■ Tricky

5. To the nearest 10m, what is the difference in altitude between the two Windyhill locations on the map?

6. Where on the map might it be said that Shakespeare rules unhappily?

■ Challenging

7. Start at a short day visible just above where seniors don't tell the truth. Go west on the road and keep on the road until you pass where Bush bushes could grow. Turn right and continue ahead the number of roundabouts equal to half the number of times the word Craig can be found on the map. Where do you finish?

8. Below are five clues with alternate letters given. Four represent places on the map – which four are they, and what places do they represent on the map?

   _I_W_O_

   _L_N_A_R_C_

   _I_H_C_R_A _O_D

   _E_F_E_D _O_S_

   _E_T_H_A_D _A_M

Map 3 OWAIN GLYNDWR AND SYCHARTH

Owain Glyndwr's rebellion was an attempt by the Welsh people to resist English rule. Despite his failure, Glyndwr remains one of Wales' most beloved heroes and a symbol of Welsh identity.

Little is known about Glyndwr's early life, but we know he was born around 1354 in the Welsh Marches, a border region between Wales and England. His parents were Anglo-Welsh gentry, and Glyndwr was educated in England and maintained his status as a noble in Wales.

Glyndwr completed three years in the English army; he fought along the Scottish border and returned to Wales in 1387. At the time, England suffered civil unrest caused by growing political and social uncertainty. Glyndwr lived in his ancestral home, Sycharth, a fortified manor house with a defensive wall and moat. It's believed that the Welsh revolt was fuelled by a land dispute between Owain and his neighbour, Baron Reynold Grey of Ruthin. Glyndwr was offended when some of his lands were seized, and the baron was not prosecuted due to his friendship with the new King Henry IV. As a result, Glyndwr took up arms against England.

The ultimate act of rebellion came on 16 September 1400, when Glyndwr was proclaimed Prince of Wales with many dignitaries in attendance. The title had been taken by the English and since 1301 it had been bestowed upon the heir apparent of the English throne. Reclaiming the title was a major symbolic gesture.

In northern Wales, Glyndwr seized settlements and his rebellion grew in strength, storming English castles and strongholds. Despite an impressive series of military victories, the Welsh simply could not compete with the size of the English military. Blockades impoverished the Welsh people and morale plummeted.

Glyndwr led his final raid in 1412, after which he disappeared, and the exact year of his death is unknown. His son Maredudd ab Owain accepted a pardon from King Henry V in 1421, formally ending the rebellion.

The story of Glyndwr remains an important part of Welsh folk history. His real life has evolved into the mythic tale of a warrior and national folk hero. Glyndwr has become the father of the Welsh nation and remains an enduring symbol of Welsh independence.

■ Easy

1. Which is the largest park on the map?

2. What label appears at the highest elevation on the map?

■ Medium

3. Which location on the map is just one letter away from BEVAN, and on which contour does it lie?

4. What is the closest distance between any two footbridges on the map, to the nearest 100m?

■ Tricky

5. At which location on the map does it sound like you might be ill for longer?

6. How many labels on the map contain words with a double letter in them? (A double letter is the same letter twice in a row in a word, such as the letter 'P' in the word 'mapping'.)

■ Challenging

7. Start in the land between Canada and Mexico. Follow the 200m contour until you are south of a farm. Head to the road directly south of that, and follow the road between two wells. At the junction, go in the direction of the European emergency number. At the next major junction, take the on-road cycle route all the way along its length. Where are you, and why might Tiger Woods be there?

8. Which places on the map are represented by the clues below? They have had their vowels removed and consonants respaced.

CDM STN YGLW YDN

NN TG CH

BLN HG FDD

BWR DD T RRR GL WY DD

Map 4 WALTER RALEIGH AND HAYES BARTON

Sir Walter Raleigh was born in 1552, in Hayes Barton, a country house near the village of East Budleigh in Devon. Records of his early life are scarce, but he came from a rich family of devout Protestants, persecuted during the brief reign of the Catholic Queen Mary. Consequently, he held a deep hatred for Catholics throughout his life.

Raleigh was educated at Oriel College, Oxford, although he never finished his degree. In 1578, he joined an expedition to North America with his half-brother Humphrey Gilbert. He was invited to court, where his adventurous spirit and handsome physique drew the attention of Queen Elizabeth I. Legend has it that Raleigh gallantly threw his cloak across a puddle so that the Queen could keep her feet dry.

Raleigh was a major figure in the exploration of the New World. He can be credited for the introduction of the potato, which has become a staple, but he can also be blamed for introducing tobacco to the world. The Queen knighted him in 1584; he was given estates in Ireland and became a Member of Parliament.

For three years Raleigh funded three separate expeditions to Roanoke Island and attempted to create a permanent colony for the English. After five years, a visiting ship found no trace of the settlers. Their disappearance could never be explained and the settlement became known as the 'Lost Colony'.

Raleigh was a prolific writer of poetry, history and political tracts, and published an account of his travels in South America, *The Discovery of Guiana* (1596).

When James I ascended the throne in 1603, Raleigh fell out of favour and was imprisoned in the Tower of London. He was released in order to lead an expedition to find the lost gold of 'El Dorado', but was captured by the Spanish.

When he returned to England, he was once again sent to the Tower. He published the first five volumes of *The History of The World* (1614), which contained some contemptuous views of the monarchy. James I and the Archbishop of Canterbury seized copies and destroyed them, but despite their greatest efforts, the book became one of the most popular publications of the seventeenth century.

Raleigh was released but offended the King one last time. He was charged with treason and executed on 29 October 1618.

QUESTIONS

■ Easy

1. How many parking symbols are there on the map?

2. Which items of kitchen equipment can be found on the map?

■ Medium

3. Are there more commons or plantations on the map, and by how many?

4. Which forest area sounds like it might have four presidents carved into it?

■ Tricky

5. What is the lowest contour present in the Danger Area?

6. Which location on the map is 4km from the Danger Area's tumulus and 2.1km from the tumuli just south of Bicton Common?

■ Challenging

7. Starting at the flying brother's way, draw a line to a place where weapons are no longer in operation. From there, draw a line to the other disused feature on the map. Once there, draw one final line to a common between a boundary stone and a car park at 118m altitude. When done correctly, a large version of a sign used on OS maps will have been drawn. What does that sign mean?

8. Piece together these words to form five locations from the map:

BIG / BY / FIRS / FISH / FOUR / HA / LANE / PONDS / STOCK / TING / TON / WOOD / YES / YET

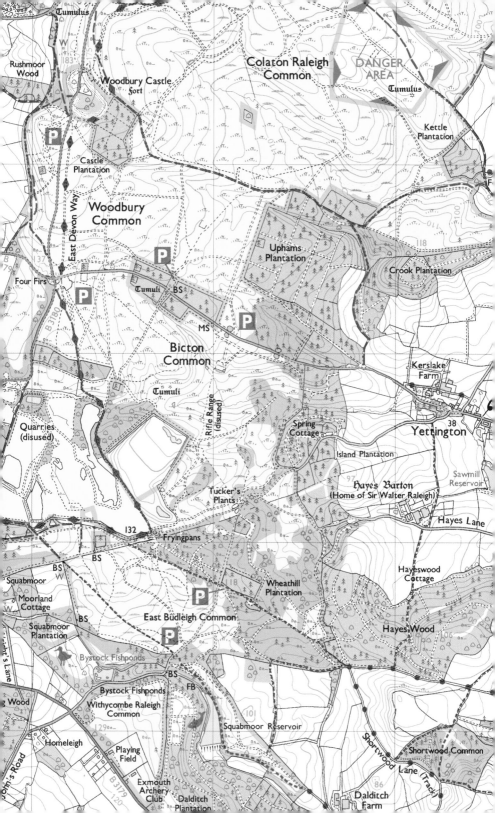

Map 5 HORATIO NELSON AND BURNHAM THORPE

Horatio Nelson was born on 29 September 1758, in Burnham Thorpe, Norfolk. His father, Edmund, was a rector, and his mother, Catherine Suckling, was the daughter of a wealthy family; Horatio was the sixth of their eleven children.

Nelson joined the Royal Navy as a midshipman at the age of twelve. He quickly rose to the rank of lieutenant by the age of twenty and saw action in the American and French Revolutionary Wars.

In his personal life, Nelson married Frances Nisbet in 1787, on the Caribbean island of Nevis. He famously had an affair with Lady Emma Hamilton, the wife of Sir William Hamilton, the British ambassador in Naples.

Nelson initially met Lady Hamilton in 1793, and then again in 1798 after his victory at the Battle of the Nile, which established his reputation worldwide. Lady Hamilton arranged a lavish fortieth birthday celebration for Nelson, then worked as his secretary. It wasn't long before gossip circulated about their romance and the affair became a public topic in English newspapers.

Professionally, Nelson was appointed commander-in-chief of the Mediterranean fleet and he led a series of successful campaigns against the French. His leadership and tactical skills were instrumental in British victories during the Napoleonic Wars. In 1805, his greatest victory occurred during the Battle of Trafalgar against the combined fleets of France and Spain. He used innovative tactics, the 'Nelson Touch', dividing the enemy line and attacking from both sides. However, Nelson was hit by a French sniper's bullet and was fatally wounded. He died on board his ship, HMS *Victory* on 21 October 1805.

Vice Admiral Nelson's death made him a national hero, and he was given a grand state funeral that lasted five days. His coffin was made from the mast of the French ship *L'Orient*, which was destroyed during his victory in the Battle of the Nile. Nelson's impressive funerary monument can be found in the south transept of St Paul's Cathedral, and Nelson's Column was erected in Trafalgar Square in 1843. His contributions to British naval history make him one of the most well-known historical public figures in Britain.

In his birthplace of Burnham Thorpe, the main public house opened in 1637. It was known as The Plough until 1798, when it was renamed 'The Lord Nelson' in honour of his victory against the French during the Battle of the Nile.

■ Easy

1. The highest point on the map lies on which road?

2. Where might a Great British Bake Off judge live?

■ Medium

3. What is the sum of the numbers in the same grid square as the well?

4. How many places of worship (marked with a +, + on a square or + on a circle) are on the map?

■ Tricky

5. What type of building on the map is in the shape of the number 4?

6. Why would a hybrid fruit, opera singer Charlotte and St Mary all have voted against Brexit?

■ Challenging

7. Start at Nelson's origin and head north on the road past a farm that's soapy without hesitations. Keep heading north on the road and turn in a sinister way when you reach an A-road. At a chicane just past a windmill, head upriver. Keep going until you reach unused tracks, and head east until you get to a region of water storage. What number have you traced out?

8. Match up these words to form four locations on the map:

   AGE / AMY'S / BE / BELL / CRAB / FARM / GRAVEL / HALL / HILL / LANE / PIT / SEW / WORKS

Map 6 ISAMBARD KINGDOM BRUNEL AND PORTSMOUTH

Isambard Kingdom Brunel was born on 9 April 1806 in Portsmouth. His father, Marc, was a French engineer who had left his homeland during the French Revolution. He spent a significant portion of his career working on naval projects in Portsmouth, and he was involved in the design and construction of the Portsmouth Block Mills, mechanised factories that produced wooden pulley blocks for the Royal Navy during the Napoleonic Wars.

Isambard had a natural talent for mathematics and learned Euclidean geometry by the age of eight. He was educated in Hove and then in Caen, France. He was then apprenticed to Abraham-Louis Breguet, one of the most eminent watchmakers and inventors of scientific instruments.

Young Brunel's first major achievement came under the supervision of his father, assisting with the planning and construction of the Thames Tunnel from Rotherhithe to Wapping. In 1831, he won a competition for his design of the Clifton Suspension Bridge across the River Avon. Brunel described it as 'my first child, my darling' and it marked a significant turning point in structural engineering. It took thirty-three years to complete the project.

In 1833, Brunel was appointed chief engineer for the Great Western Railway and began work on a line that would link London to Bristol. His network of individually designed tunnels, viaducts and impressive bridges was an outstanding achievement, culminating in Bristol Temple Meads station.

Brunel is also famous for designing several famous ships. The SS *Great Western* was the first transatlantic steamship, launched in 1837, and the SS *Great Britain* was launched in 1843, the world's first iron-hulled, screw-propelled, seafaring ship. He also collaborated with John Scott Russell to design the SS *Great Eastern*, which was the biggest ship ever built at that point in time. Brunel also redesigned some of Britain's most important docks: Bristol, Cardiff, Monkwearmouth and Milford Haven. He was a skilled project manager who could oversee every part of his plan from design to construction, all the way through to operation.

Towards the end of his life, Brunel was involved in the design of the Royal Albert Bridge which spans the River Tamar between Devon and Cornwall, one of his most notable engineering achievements.

Brunel's contributions to the field of engineering had an immense impact on the modern world. He died of a stroke on 15 September 1859. He was only fifty-three years old.

QUESTIONS

■ Easy

1. What letter is located at the intersection of two streets that share their names with chess pieces?

2. Where might the army have an argument?

■ Medium

3. Which location on the map is an anagram of SMALL BRICK DRAMA?

4. Where might David Walliams and Matt Lucas have filmed a sitcom?

■ Tricky

5. Where might you stalk a pantomime character, if they were missing jazz's Fitzgerald?

6. To the nearest 50m, what is the distance between the two triangulation points?

■ Challenging

7. How many pubs are marked on the map?

8. Which three letters of the alphabet are not present at all on the map?

Map 7 DAVID STIRLING AND THE BRIDGE OF ALLAN

Sir Archibald 'David' Stirling was a British Army officer who founded the Special Air Service during World War II. Born in his ancestral home, Keir House in Perthshire, Stirling came from a prestigious family of baronets and could trace his ancestry back to Charles II.

Stirling attended Ampleforth College and then Trinity College, Cambridge, but he was thrown out after his first year. Having been a member of the Officer Training Corps in Ampleforth, Stirling volunteered in 1940 and joined No. 8 Commando, who were already active in the Middle East. The British troops had suffered heavy casualties in the region, and Stirling was convinced that a team of specialist soldiers would stand a better chance of breaking the German supply line if they attacked from the desert at night.

After finagling a meeting with Sir Claude Auchinleck, the Regional Commander in Chief, Stirling was permitted to form a special operations unit in 1941. The original name of the parachute unit was a hoax dreamt up by Dudley Clarke, a master of military deception. 'L Detachment, Special Air Service Brigade' was an imaginary force he had created to divert the attention of enemy spies in the area.

The first parachute attack, organised to hit a German airfield, was thwarted by desert storms that blew the plane off course. Out of the original intake of fifty-five men, only twenty-one survived the mission unscathed. The unit regrouped and Stirling organised land-based airfield raids, using American jeeps armed with Vickers K machine guns and handheld incendiary devices, Lewes bombs. Stirling and his men conducted numerous hit-and-run missions, raiding airfields and destroying over 250 warplanes. In 1942, Stirling was captured, and after several escapes, he was detained in Colditz Castle for the rest of the war.

The SAS became one of the most renowned and effective special forces units in military history. Stirling led the SAS on numerous missions in North Africa, Italy and France and was known for his ingenuity, tenacity and incredible bravery.

Awarded the Distinguished Service Order in 1942, Stirling was also appointed an Officer of the Order of the British Empire in 1946, and a Knight Bachelor in 1990 for services to the military.

Stirling died on 4 November 1990. A memorial statue by Angela Conner is on the B824, on the edge of the Keir estate.

■ Easy

1. The southernmost symbol for a golf course lies between which two height contours?

2. Travelling as the crow flies from Lower Taylorton to Westleys, how many times do you cross the River Forth?

■ Medium

3. Which location on the map looks like an imperial unit of distance has stumbled?

4. To the nearest 500m, what is the greatest east–west distance between the M9 and the A9 on the map?

■ Tricky

5. Travelling only by A-roads, B-roads or motorways, what is the minimum number of roundabouts one would have to traverse to get from the University of Stirling to King's Knot?

6. Which location on the map becomes the name of a fictional school for girls if one letter is replaced with 'TR'?

■ Challenging

7. Which of these is the odd one out?

   – Memorial to Gromit's owner

   – French strength

   – Rook, in chess

   – Reputation of 14lb

8. Which locations are represented by the clues below that have had their vowels removed and consonants respaced? One is a red herring and does not correspond to a place on the map – which is it?

   BR SD

   LGV LL

   PRK FKR

   SK CH

   RTH RYC STL

   STR LN GM SS

William Wilberforce and
Kingston upon Hull

T E Lawrence
and Tremadog

Winston Churchill and
Blenheim Palace

Robert Smallbones and
Trinity College, Oxford

Benjamin Disraeli and
Hughenden Manor

POLITICAL CHALLENGERS

8. *William Wilberforce*

———

9. *Benjamin Disraeli*

———

10. *Winston Churchill*

———

11. *Robert Smallbones*

———

12. *T E Lawrence*

Map 8 WILLIAM WILBERFORCE AND KINGSTON UPON HULL

William Wilberforce was a prominent British politician and philanthropist who played a significant role in the abolition of the slave trade within the British Empire.

Wilberforce was born in a merchant's house on the high street in Kingston upon Hull on 24 August 1759. He was the only son of a wealthy merchant, Robert Wilberforce, and his wife Elizabeth Bird. His grandfather William had made some of the family fortune refining sugar imported from plantations in the West Indies, where the industry relied on the forced labour of enslaved Africans.

After the death of his father, Young William Wilberforce spent time in Wimbledon with extended family. He returned to be educated at Hull Grammar School before attending St John's College, Cambridge, at the age of seventeen. The death of his grandfather left him independently wealthy, and he gained both a Bachelor of Arts in 1781 and a Master of Arts in 1788.

During university, he befriended William Pitt, and the two would often watch the debate in the House of Commons. In 1780, Wilberforce was elected as the Member of Parliament for Hull, and he represented the city for twenty-five years. He used his position in Parliament to actively campaign against the slave trade. The Abolition of Slave Trade Act 1807 came about because of Wilberforce's efforts, making it illegal to engage in slave trade in the transatlantic region. It was not until the Slavery Abolition Act of 1833 that slavery was abolished within the entirety of the British Empire.

In 1833, he suffered a serious bout of influenza and never fully recovered. William Wilberforce died on 29 July 1833 at his cousin's home in Cadogan Place, London. He was honoured with a burial at Westminster Abbey, in the north transept next to his great friend William Pitt.

▨ Easy

1. Considering only the area common to both maps, which bridge is present on the new map but not on the old?

2. Hull College has been built on land partly reclaimed from which feature?

▨ Medium

3. Why is Salthouse Lane likely to have been given that name?

4. Where might you find an envious Spice Girl?

▨ Tricky

5. When comparing maps, how does Charlotte set herself free?

6. What connects black gold, a horror-film franchise that began in 2004, a mythological bird and the location of a Wonderful library?

▨ Challenging

7. Going from car park to car park, go in straight lines from the one nearest to the River Hull to the one furthest from the River Hull to the one furthest from the River Humber to the one nearest the River Humber. How many more times do you cross water marked on the map compared to the number you have just traced?

8. Which street names (ignoring words like street, lane, road, etc.) could be hinted at by the following?

    – The fifth mole

    – Take command of a place to live

    – Flank of an armed force

    – Somewhere for William and Harry to alight

    – Secure a golf club

    – Potato

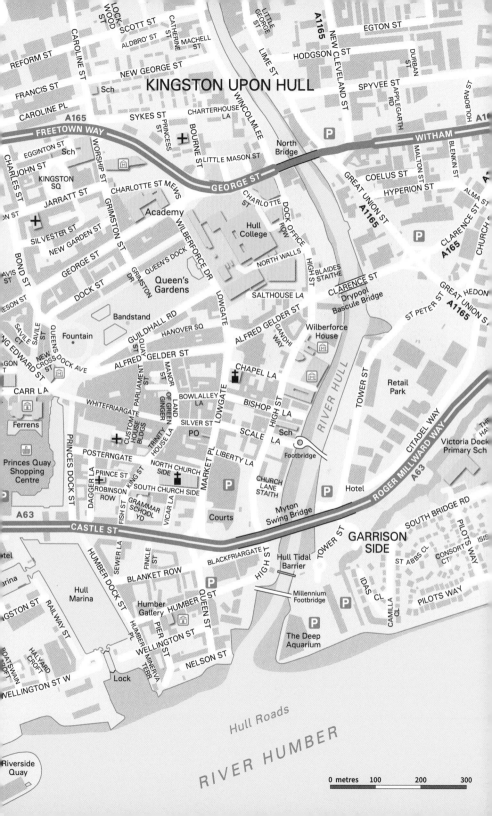

Map 9 BENJAMIN DISRAELI AND HUGHENDEN MANOR

Benjamin Disraeli was born in Bloomsbury, London, on 21 December 1804. His Jewish father Isaac was a scholar and literary critic. After a disagreement with his synagogue, Isaac left Judaism and the family converted to Anglicanism when Benjamin was twelve. As a Jew, young Benjamin would never have had a career in politics, but this conversion would open up future opportunities.

Before he had any interest in becoming a politician, Disraeli was an accomplished writer. He continued to publish novels, poetry, plays and works of non-fiction throughout his life.

In 1837, Disraeli was elected to represent Maidstone, and then Shrewsbury in 1841. As Member of Parliament for Buckinghamshire, Disraeli purchased Hughenden Manor in 1848, borrowing heavily to afford the country seat. Once he had acquired the 750-acre estate, he had everything he needed to become a prominent political figure. In 1852, Prime Minister Lord Derby offered him the position of Chancellor of the Exchequer, but Disraeli's disastrous budget led to the government's downfall. In 1868, when Derby resigned due to ill health, he asked Disraeli to form a government. This short stint as prime minister resulted in some notable legislation. Despite this progress, he was defeated at the next general election.

As an opposition leader, Disraeli enjoyed scathing debates across the dispatch box with Prime Minister William Ewart Gladstone. He was a well-regarded statesman during his time in office, a man who could connect with all manner of people. Disraeli worked hard to transform the Conservative Party into a party that would appeal to working-class people.

At the age of seventy, Disraeli became prime minister once again in 1874. He paved the way for social and political reforms by improving working environments and introducing the Public Health Act of 1875, which improved sanitation and living conditions for many people. In terms of foreign policy, Disraeli was instrumental in Britain's acquisition of shares in the Suez Canal Company, a strategic move that secured British influence in the Middle East. In 1879, Queen Victoria made him 1st Earl of Beaconsfield and Disraeli took the opportunity to lead from the House of Lords. However, the Liberals won the election in 1880.

Disraeli died in London after a bout of bronchitis on 19 April 1881. He left instructions that he was not to be given a state funeral, to honour a promise made to his wife Mary-Anne. Instead, he was buried beside her at Hughenden Church.

▇ Easy

1. How many schools are indicated on the map?

2. What is researched and developed somewhere on the map?

▇ Medium

3. If you travel from one allotment gardens to the other as the crow flies, how many footpaths or bridleways do you cross?

4. Which road has a name that would be a part of the body if the letter 'L' was inserted into it somewhere?

▇ Tricky

5. Multiply the number of farms by the number of woods. What number is the result?

6. Which of these is the odd one out: Phil, Hugh, Adam, Mo, Warren?

▇ Challenging

7. Start at a point 1m below a perfect three-dart score in elevation close to actor Helen's rise. Proceed northeast on a road until you reach a roundabout, and take the first exit. Turn right just after a pub, then head along a road you might put on your legs. Go downhill until you're 60m lower than your starting elevation. What letter have you traced out?

8. Which locations on the map are represented by the phrases given below? Only alternate letters for each place are given.

    _O_M_E'_ O_C_A_D_

    _I_D_E _O_G_

    _O_G_O_E _L_N_A_I_N_

    _P_R_S _R_U_D

    _O_N_E_ C_M_O_

Map 10 WINSTON CHURCHILL AND BLENHEIM PALACE

A soldier, writer, and prime minister of Great Britain twice, Winston Leonard Spencer Churchill was born in Blenheim Palace, Oxfordshire in 1874, to Lord Randolph Churchill and Jennie Jerome. Churchill had a private education, then entered the British Army to serve in the Boer War and World War I. During his military service he pursued a career in journalism, becoming a war correspondent and proving himself an influential communicator.

Churchill married Clementine Hozier in 1908, and their long and happy marriage provided a firm foundation for his political career during which he served in various high-profile positions: as a Member of Parliament for five different constituencies, as a cabinet minister for the Board of Trade, as Home Secretary and then as First Lord of the Admiralty. Churchill had a sharp wit that would amuse his political opponents as much as his supporters. In 1940, after the resignation of Neville Chamberlain, Churchill succeeded him as prime minister of a coalition government. He played a crucial role in World War II, leading Britain with his powerful speeches and resoluteness. He became a symbol of British courage and determination.

After the war, Churchill faced political defeats but maintained his position as a statesman in terms of global politics. He played a key role in shaping post-war Europe, and his vision for a united Europe became the basis for the European Union. Despite his numerous achievements and mass popularity, Churchill was not without controversy. A staunch imperialist and monarchist, he faced criticism for his views on race and his colonial policies.

Churchill's legacy is one of extraordinary leadership and resilience during a time of crisis, and his indomitable spirit continues to represent British bravery and fortitude. His birthplace, Blenheim Palace, is situated near the village of Woodstock. It is a stunning example of baroque architecture, sprawled across two thousand acres. The formal gardens and grounds were landscaped by Capability Brown and feature a private lake, fed by the River Glyme.

■ Easy

1. What do the Rose Garden (on a path going south from Blenheim Palace), Walnut Clump and a building near High Park's reservoir have in common?

2. On which street in Woodstock is there a church with a tower?

■ Medium

3. One feature has different three-word names on the two maps. What are those names?

4. What connects Combe, Burleigh and Thatch?

■ Tricky

5. How is blonde actor Pike doing?

6. To the nearest 250m, how far apart are the two museums on the new map?

■ Challenging

7. Starting at a septet of spanners, follow water around until you meet a £1,000 spanner. Travel on the National Trail ahead of you until you reach 67,760 square yard cluster. Turn left at the altitude marker and keep going until you reach another altitude marker 10m higher. What letter have you traced out?

8. Match up these words to make the names of six locations on the maps:

CLUMP / COLUMN / DOG / FIR / HALL / HILL / HOUSE / ICE / IN / ION / KENNEL / MARY / MISS / OF / PARK / STREET / VICTORY

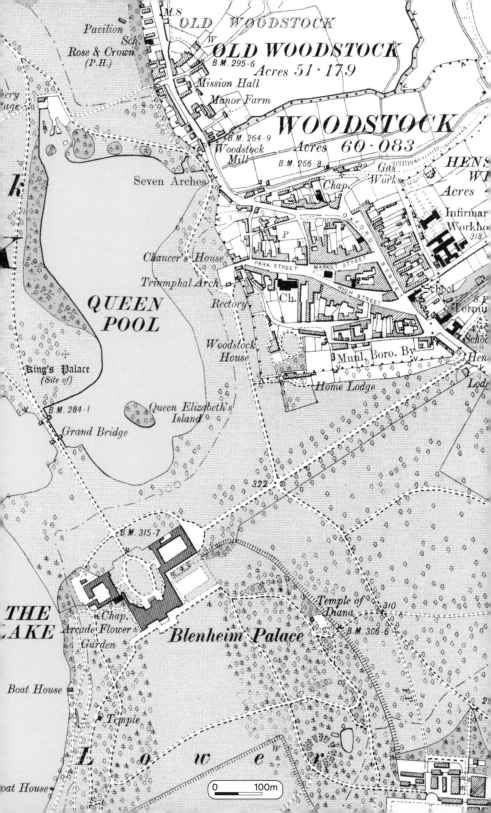

Map 11 ROBERT SMALLBONES AND TRINITY COLLEGE, OXFORD

Robert Townsend Smallbones was born in Vienna, Austria in 1884. His parents emigrated to Britain and he attended Trinity College, Oxford, where he gained a Master of Arts degree before joining the Foreign Office in 1910. In 1932, the Foreign Office sent him to Germany, and by 1938 he was the British Consul-General in Frankfurt. Throughout those years, Smallbones witnessed the rise of the Nazis and repeatedly warned the Foreign Office about the situation that was developing in Germany.

On 9 November 1938, the Nazis rampaged through Frankfurt in a coordinated wave of anti-Semitic violence that came to be known as Kristallnacht. Desperate, the local Jews came to the Consulate for help, but Smallbones was in England. His wife and mother opened the gates, and it became a refuge for the Jewish community in Frankfurt.

Britain's Home Office did not want mass immigration, but Smallbones convinced them to allow Jews with US visas to enter and wait for safe passage to America. He informed Jewish leaders that families could apply on behalf of anyone who had already been sent to a concentration camp. He also visited concentration camps and demanded the release of Jewish people, coming face to face with the Gestapo and never backing down.

Smallbones and his staff worked tirelessly to attain travel visas for persecuted Jews. When war was declared and he returned to England, around 48,000 visas had been issued. The entire operation was kept quiet, for fear of public reaction if they knew how many people had been allowed into the country. But the Gestapo knew and his name appeared in their 'black book', so if the Nazis had ever succeeded in invading Britain, they would have killed him.

Robert Smallbones retired in 1945, and he and his wife settled in São Paulo, Brazil. He died on 29 May 1976. In 2008, the British government officially acknowledged Smallbones's heroic efforts. In 2013, he was posthumously honoured as a 'Holocaust Hero' in London and Frankfurt.

QUESTIONS

■ Easy

1. Which college owns buildings with this shape?

2. Which street connects Merton Street to the High Street and is labelled on one map but not the other?

■ Medium

3. A = number of places of worship with a tower

   B = number of places of worship with a spire, minaret or dome

   C = number of places of worship WITHOUT a tower, spire, minaret or dome

   Looking at the new map, what number is (A x B) + C?

4. I used to be 423. Which three numbers am I now?

■ Tricky

5. Find somewhere in southwest Wales where might you go for an argument.

6. Which city connects to a French 'handsome mountain' and a common pub name multiplied by itself?

■ Challenging

7. On the new map, draw lines between the locations listed below. If a location is on the old map, work out its equivalent position on the new map. What creature is at the cross?

   – An extremely cold quayside to the old nunnery corner of a road belonging to an animated TV comedy.

   – A former *The Late Late Show* host's piece of moon to an occidental book store.

8. Which places on the maps are represented by the following clues that have had their vowels removed and consonants respaced?

   RS KNC LLG

   LBR TST RT

   PT TRV RS

   GSS TRT

   NWC LL GSC HL

   RL CL LG

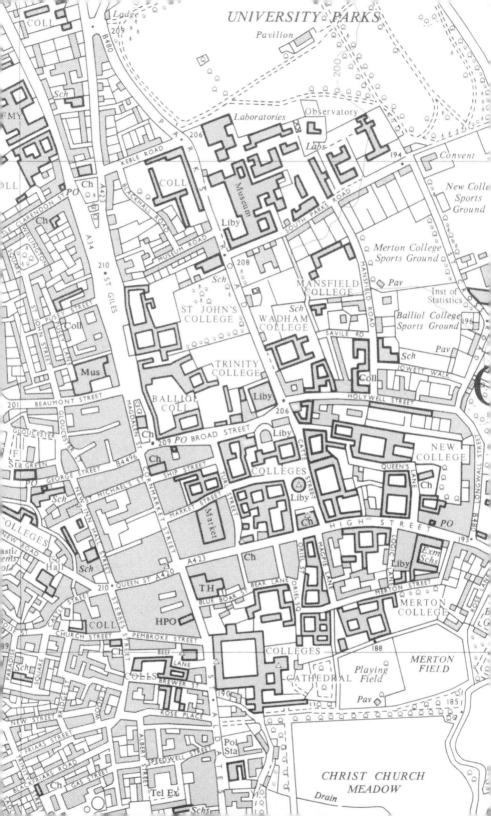

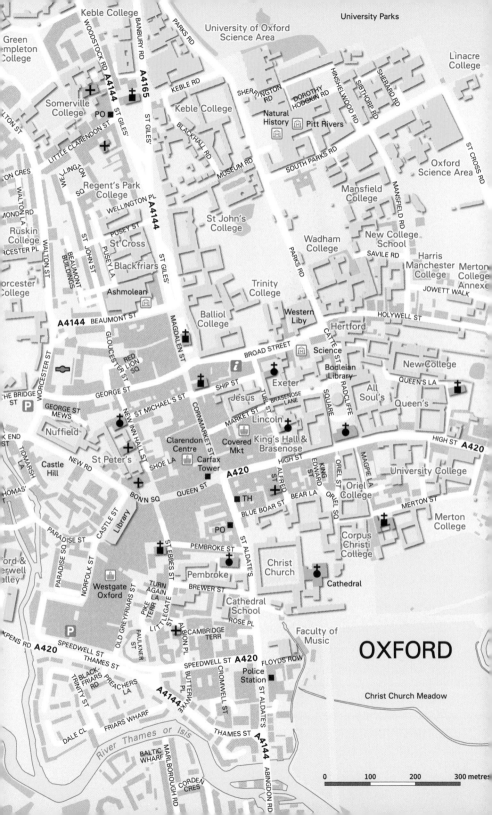

Map 12 TE LAWRENCE AND TREMADOG

Known as 'Lawrence of Arabia', this British colonel was a key figure in the Arab revolt and a significant contributor to the British war effort in the Middle East during World War I.

Thomas Edward Lawrence was born in Tremadog on 16 August 1888, the third son of Thomas Chapman and Sarah Junner. When the Lawrence family lived in Tremadog, their house was called Gorphwysfa, Welsh for resting place. Now known as Snowdon Lodge, the building operates as a hostel for hikers and climbers. The lodge is full of information and memorabilia, and outside a blue plaque commemorates the birthplace of TE Lawrence.

At the age of twenty-two, Lawrence learned Arabic whilst working as an archaeologist in Beirut. The British Army employed him provisionally to map the Negev Desert, a land of strategic importance that lay between British-ruled Egypt and the Ottoman Empire.

Lawrence worked as a liaison officer between the British government and the Arab tribes and aided the Arab revolt against the Ottoman Empire from 1916 until 1918. Lawrence stayed with the local people, spoke their language and wore their robes so they would accept him as a leader. His expertise in guerrilla warfare and his understanding of the culture, customs and politics of the Arab world helped build an effective relationship with Emir Faisal, the son of Sharif Hussein of Mecca.

In 1922, Lawrence published his memoir, *Seven Pillars of Wisdom*, which provides a vivid account of his exploits in the desert. The book outlines his deep admiration for the Arab people and their struggle for independence. The manuscript was the basis of the 1962 film *Lawrence of Arabia*, which was directed by David Lean and starred Peter O'Toole. It is still considered a masterpiece of modern cinema.

Lawrence spent a lot of time at Clouds Hill, a remote rural cottage in Dorset, and he planned to retire there. He was great friends with Thomas Hardy and would regularly ride his Brough Superior motorbike to Hardy's home near Dorchester. Two months into his retirement, on 19 May 1935, Lawrence was killed when he swerved to avoid two boys on bicycles and his motorbike hit a tree.

Clouds Hill is run by the National Trust and the interior has been kept exactly as Lawrence left it, complete with furniture, books and photographs of his time in Arabia.

■ Easy

1. What exciting activity can be found somewhere along the A498?

2. What is the lowest altitude measured, at several individual points, on the map?

■ Medium

3. How many railway stations are there on the map?

4. What is the distance, to the nearest 500m, between the highest peaks on either side of the Afon Glaslyn? (They may not be directly next to the Afon Glaslyn.)

■ Tricky

5. How many marsh symbols (like this) are present on the land mass in the south of the map?

6. Which location on the map contains the name of a sport written backwards?

■ Challenging

7. Start at a campsite without a caravan park. Head west on the main road, and at the roundabout take the first available exit that results in your road number changing. At the next roundabout, take the first main exit if there is one cemetery marked on the map, or take the second main exit if there are two cemeteries. Continue through a line of four buildings of the same type. Travel on this road for just over 2km. Where are you now?

8. Which labels on the map are the following phrases anagrams of? Beware, one is a red herring. Which one is it?

SAW RERUN

THOR GETS BY

IMPORT ORE IN

WEASEL VOWEL

WOLF HUNG LYCRA

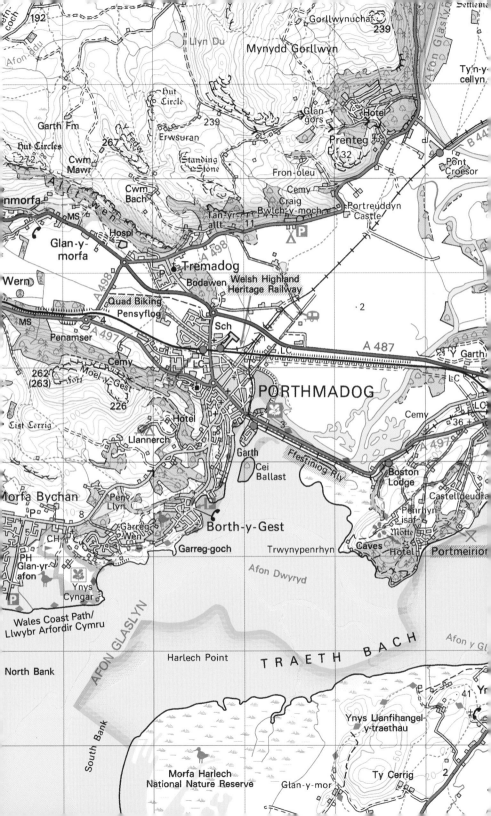

HOW TO SPOT HISTORY ON A MAP

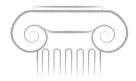

When you look at an Ordnance Survey map – online, on the OS Maps app or on an OS paper map – there are lots of symbols, each describing different features. Some of these can reveal the hidden history of a place and the more you understand the map symbols, the language of the map, the more it can tell you.

STANDING OUT IN THE LANDSCAPE

Symbols for places of worship, such as cathedrals and churches, are fantastic to navigate by and you can use the symbols on the map to tell you what to look out for. Their tall towers and elegant spires make them easy to see from afar.

 This indicates the church has a tower. Saxons usually built wooden churches – if they did build any part in stone, it was the tower. These very old church towers are round. When the Normans arrived in 1066, they rebuilt many churches in stone – their towers are usually made of very thick stone, with tiny windows and rounded doorway arches. Later medieval churches have taller towers, or sometimes levels were built on top of earlier, shorter towers.

This shows the place of worship either has a spire, minaret or dome. In the British countryside, chances are you're looking for a spire on a Christian church. Spires were constructed from 1200 onwards, in an architectural style known as 'Gothic'.

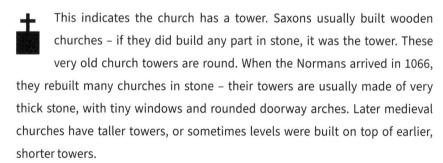 This is a place of worship with no tower or spire. These might be chapels or meeting houses, where the architecture is a lot more domestic in style, representing a different style of worship.

𝔊𝔬𝔱𝔥𝔦𝔠 𝔰𝔠𝔯𝔦𝔭𝔱 𝔬𝔫 𝔪𝔞𝔭𝔰

When you see a Gothic label on the map, it means the site is definitely archaeological, but one that isn't Roman. The feature will usually be prehistoric (i.e. before AD 43), or medieval (from the 400s AD until around 1600), or slightly later.

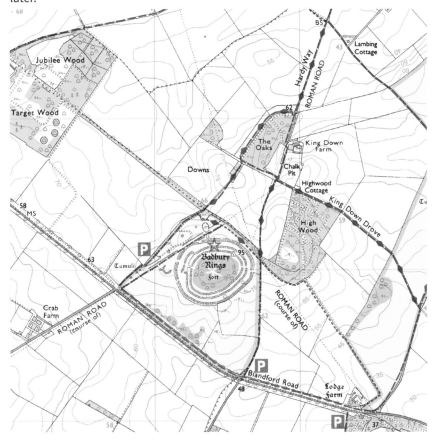

Many ancient historic sites are on open access land and can be explored, such as this hill fort at Badbury Rings in Dorset. The mounds marked as Tumuli are Bronze Age while the hill fort is Iron Age. Lodge Farm, to the south east of Badbury Rings, is medieval.

NATURAL OR BY HUMAN HAND?

The brown contour lines on a map indicate the natural rise and fall of the land. They show the height of hills and the steepness of valleys. Where people have reshaped land for their own ends, for a hill fort or railway embankment for example, then this effort is recorded with the triangular hachure symbol.

The triangular shape indicates the direction of the slope – the narrow end always faces downhill. They help reveal our ancient landscape and archaeologists use the symbol to record field systems and settlements, as well as mounds, ditches and other low earthworks.

A mound may be an ancient burial mound (also sometimes labelled as 'Tumulus' or plural 'Tumuli' on the map). It may be a burnt mound of stones that was possibly used in prehistoric times for cooking, or it could be a pillow mound, which is a manmade medieval rabbit warren.

ROMAN ROADS ON A MAP

If a stretch of road or an earthwork has been confirmed as being originally Roman, it'll be marked in capitals, in a sans serif font. Sometimes you'll see one section of Roman road marked, but then the modern road curves away elsewhere. Look on the map to see if you can trace the original route of the Roman road – it's sometimes preserved in field boundaries, minor roads, footpaths or parish boundaries. You may be able to trace it to another section marked ROMAN ROAD.

At least 10,000 miles (16,000km) of Roman road were built in Britain, mostly before AD 150, and they used the existing network of earth tracks and routes that the Iron Age Britons used. It's a myth that Roman roads were dead straight, regardless of the terrain – they were more pragmatic than that.

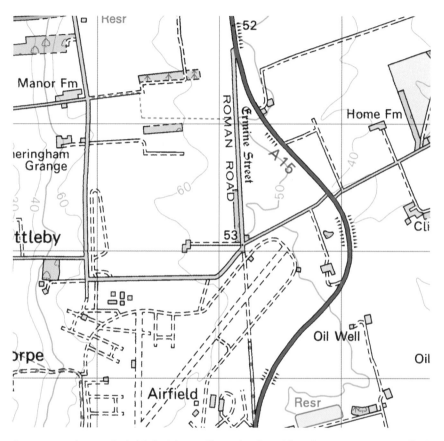

Roman roads are straight, but in sections. Look out for clues on your map that might show where Roman surveyors decided to change direction in order to reduce the gradient up hills or to avoid obstacles.

The main road north from Lincoln, the A15, is remarkably straight for many for many miles, following a Roman road which in medieval times became known as Ermine Street. You can see where the modern road has had to go around an extended runway – the story features in our *Puzzle Tour of Britain* book.

The Edinburgh Seven

Elizabeth Barrett
Browning and Coxhoe

Betsi Cadwaladr
and Llanycil

Nye Bevan and Tredegar

Alice Seeley Harris
and Malmesbury, Wilts

HEALTH AND SOCIAL REFORMERS

13. *Betsi Cadwaladr*

14. *Elizabeth Barrett Browning*

15. *Alice Seeley Harris*

16. *Nye Bevan*

17. *The Edinburgh Seven*

Map 13 BETSI CADWALADR
AND LLANYCIL

One of sixteen children, Elizabeth 'Betsi' Cadwaladr was born in Llanycil, near Bala, in Wales on 24 May 1789. Her father was a Methodist preacher and her mother died when she was only five years old.

Cadwaladr spent her early years working as a domestic maid, which provided her with the opportunity to learn English and travel widely. Records show that she often used the name Davis, perhaps because it is far easier to spell and pronounce than her Welsh name. She became a maid to a ship's captain and sailed the world, visiting South America, Africa and Australia and meeting interesting people along the way. During these expeditions, she learned how to tend to the sick and injured and deliver babies.

Cadwaladr left it late in life to train as a nurse, but she qualified at age sixty-five and fought very hard to serve in the military nursing service in Crimea. She frequently clashed ideals with Florence Nightingale, a woman thirty-one years younger, from a very privileged background and who was a stickler for bureaucracy.

Cadwaladr often bent the rules and used her initiative, being a more intuitive nurse. The antagonism between the two women was so awful, Cadwaladr moved to a hospital behind the front lines in Balaclava, rather than work with Nurse Nightingale. However, there was a grudging acknowledgment from the younger nurse, who respected Cadwaladr's skill in improving some of the dreadful, unhygienic conditions.

Eventually, Cadwaladr caught cholera and returned to London in 1855. She lived with her sister and spent time writing her biography, *The Autobiography of Elizabeth Davis* (1857). She died on 17 July 1860.

In 2005, the Royal College of Nursing finally proposed that Wales should acknowledge Cadwaladr as one of the pioneers of nursing, and acknowledge her considerable achievements.

The Betsi Cadwaladr University Health Board is the largest health organisation in Wales, responsible for delivering healthcare to 700,000 people, coordinating doctors' surgeries, dental services, optometry and pharmacies across North Wales.

In 2014, a poll in the *Western Mail* asked people to vote for their Welsh hero. Cadwaladr was voted number 38, ahead of Ryan Giggs, Anthony Hopkins and even Tom Jones!

QUESTIONS

▓ Easy

1. What is the Welsh word for railway?

2. What comes next in this sequence?

   169, 166, 178, 168, ??

▓ Medium

3. Where might Romeo and Juliet go for a walk?

4. Which place on the map begins with a prefix meaning 'five' and ends in an animal?

▓ Tricky

5. Including the lake depth contours, how many different heights and depths are written on the map's contour labels? (Only count repeated heights/depths once.)

6. Cerrig-llwydion and Llangower Point are less than 1km away from each other. But, staying on the map and using A-roads and B-roads, what distance do you have to travel to get from one to the other? Answer to the nearest kilometre.

▓ Challenging

7. Start at the Natural Resources Wales symbol that is in a grid square with no letters written in it. Travel in a straight line to the nearest railway station, then go directly to the 38th US president. Travel upstream past one set of weirs until you reach another weir. Travel in a straight line to a high point that, if its height is anything to go by, has all-round views. What number have you traced out?

8. Which locations and features on the map are represented by the clues below, in which only their alternate letters have been given?

   _A_T_M_R_H

   _O_T _W_W_L-_-L_Y_

   _A_T _A_H_S_

   _W_S_A_R_S

   _O_E_ Y _A_A

   _O_N_L_U

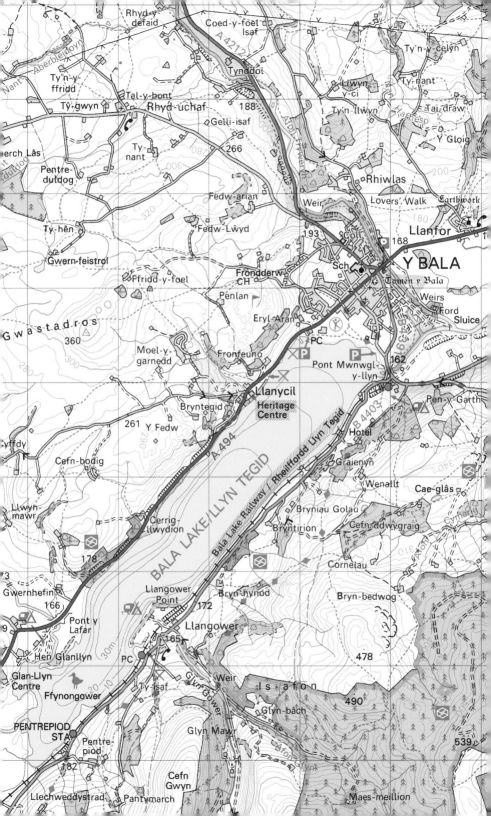

Map 14 ELIZABETH BARRETT BROWNING AND COXHOE

Elizabeth Barrett was the eldest of twelve children, born on 6 March 1806 to a prominent family in Coxhoe Hall, County Durham. From an early age, she had an aptitude for writing and received an extensive education for a woman of that era. Her early work was influenced by Wordsworth, Shelley and the Romantic poets.

In 1826, Elizabeth fell seriously ill, and her health remained fragile for the rest of her life. At this point in history, opiates were commonly prescribed for pain, and her dependence on laudanum may account for some of the more vivid depictions in her poetry. Despite her issues with chronic illness, she continued to write and gained recognition for the emotional intensity of her work. Her collection *The Seraphim, and Other Poems* (1838) and *Poems* (1844) gained critical acclaim.

Elizabeth often used poetry to broach political issues, women's rights, the abolition of slavery and child labour. Her poem, The Cry of the Children, (1843) drew attention to the plight of working juveniles and the treatment of minors, and may have positively influenced labour reforms in Victorian Britain.

In 1846, Elizabeth defied her father and eloped with Robert Browning after a secret long-distance courtship. They married at St Marylebone Parish Church and honeymooned in Paris. After the wedding, her father cut her out of the Barrett family.

The couple settled in Florence, Italy, where Elizabeth gained her strength. At the age of forty-three, she gave birth to a son, Robert Wiedeman Barrett Browning, known as 'Pen'. The Brownings became quite famous and spent their time with popular writers George Sand, Harriet Beecher Stowe and William Makepeace Thackeray, to name a few. *Sonnets from the Portuguese* (1850) is considered Elizabeth's most famous work, mainly due to the inclusion of deeply personal love sonnets addressed to her husband.

In 1860, they moved to Siena and Elizabeth became preoccupied with Italian politics, eventually publishing *Poems Before Congress* (1860), which detailed her feelings about Risorgimento, the unification of Italy. The publication caused outrage in England and damaged her reputation.

The Brownings returned to Florence, but Elizabeth's health deteriorated and she died on 29 June 1861 in the arms of her beloved husband Robert.

Coxhoe Hall was demolished in the 1950s; however, nearby St Helen's Church in Kelloe has a plaque to commemorate Elizabeth's baptism on 10 February 1808.

■ Easy

1. How many nature reserves, represented by blue ducks, are present on the map?

2. Where might an archer set fire to his weapon?

■ Medium

3. What is the sum of all the numbers in the entire row of grid squares that contains Old Quarrington?

4. What is the longest place name on the map that has no repeated letters in its name? (London has a repeated 'N' in its name, for instance.)

■ Tricky

5. What colour is Catherine?

6. What is the highest altitude measured at a point on the map?

■ Challenging

7. Start at a roundabout and mast west of a farm. Travel northwest, taking the second exit at the first roundabout you come to. Go past another mast, and turn left on to an A-road. At the first roundabout, take the first exit. At the second roundabout, take the second main exit. Stop at a letter on the road. What label is on your left?

8. Which places on the map are indicated by these cryptic clues?

   – Angry dragon saw my place to live

   – Hamlet sounds like a tree in a shelter

   – Some orcas, so pretty in a village!

   – Spanner made of iron, say, initially gladly guarded by wife-to-be

   – Visibly point at road

Map 15 ALICE SEELEY HARRIS
AND MALMESBURY, WILTSHIRE

Alice Seeley was born in Malmesbury, Wiltshire, on 24 May 1870. She trained as a teacher but became a missionary who witnessed and photographed horrific abuse in the Congo, committed during the rule of King Leopold II of Belgium.

In 1865, Leopold ascended the throne after the death of his father. He inherited the Congo Free State, which contained plentiful rubber plantations. In the late 1880s, Dunlop invented the inflatable rubber tyre and after the creation of the bicycle, there was a huge increase in demand for rubber. In order to make money and harvest the rubber, King Leopold needed labourers to work on the plantations. This was the beginning of a regime that used vile methods of forced labour, including the mutilation, rape and murder of the Congolese people.

Alice met her future husband Reverend John Harris in 1894. They married on 6 May 1898 and left for Africa four days later on the SS *Cameroon*.

In Africa, Alice taught English and John held religious services. The plantations were run by soldiers and overseers and it soon became apparent that locals were being punished if they didn't produce enough rubber in a day. Alice began to take photographs of the native people. It wasn't long before she captured images of whiplashed backs, brutal beatings and evidence of exploitation.

One of her seminal photographs was taken when a local man passed by her home, carrying the hand and foot of his daughter wrapped in a plantain leaf. Alice sat him on the stoop and took a clear photo of him staring at the unwrapped body parts. This was the image that drew the world's attention to the violence occurring in the Congo.

The Harrises also gathered eyewitness accounts of the abuse of the Congolese people which they presented to the British Foreign Office and other worldwide authorities. Their brave work and international condemnation helped to bring about change, and the brutal regime ended in 1908. It is estimated that around 10 million Congolese were murdered during this colonial period.

Alice's photographs and the accompanying documentation are now recognised as important historical records of the atrocities committed in the Congo, and she has been formally acknowledged as a human rights activist.

Alice Seeley Harris died in Lockner Holt in Guildford, Surrey, on 24 November 1970; she was one hundred years old.

■ Easy

1. What kind of building on the map has this shape?
2. Are there more labelled farms to the north of the River Avon or to the south?

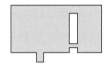

■ Medium

3. What can be found at the top of Cam's Hill?
4. What literally connects one 'Residence Ranch' to another 'Residence Ranch'?

■ Tricky

5. In relation to the map, what connects:

   (a) A bull's counterpart

   (b) Joan from *Mad Men* or a women's prison closed in 2016

   (c) Part of the body or to support financially?

6. What feature on the map could literally be represented by WARY ALI?

■ Challenging

7. Travel as the crow flies from the home of Perrin's partner to a converter of energy from the sun. Then continue as the crow flies to the name of a Scandinavian country if it was made plural and a letter 'N' was removed.

   During this journey, how many times do you cross water?

8. Five of the following are anagrams of places on the map. Where are they anagrams of, and which one is the odd one out?

   RIFLE AID

   HER RED RING

   SMALL VINO

   FOREARM COPS

   MENU: ICE GINGERSNAP

   ALL THE BEST IN DRY RUG

Map 16 NYE BEVAN AND TREDEGAR

Aneurin Bevan was born on 15 November 1897 at 32 Charles Street in Tredegar, Monmouthshire. The son of a coal miner and a seamstress, 'Nye' grew up in poverty and was surrounded by hardship. As a small boy, he suffered from a debilitating stammer and took solitary walks around Tredegar to practise talking aloud.

At the age of fourteen, Bevan worked in the coal mine with his father. By nineteen, he was heavily involved in union politics and elected head of his Miners' Lodge. In 1926, Bevan was a leading figure in the general strike; he then joined the Labour Party and was elected as MP for Ebbw Vale in 1929.

Bevan overcame his childhood speech impediment and became a strong orator; many consider him one of the finest political speakers in British history. During World War II, he was extremely critical of Winston Churchill and David Lloyd George and used his rhetorical skills in Parliament. After the war, Bevan was chosen as Minister of Health at the age of forty-seven, the youngest member of Clement Attlee's Cabinet.

The Circle is the hub of Tredegar town and home to one of its most enduring landmarks. The town clock was built in 1858 and stands 22 metres (72 feet) high, constructed of cast iron to represent the importance of iron production to the local community. This is where the town assembled to celebrate major events and hold political rallies and gatherings. Bevan delivered speeches here on many occasions.

Number 10, The Circle, was the home of The Tredegar Medical Aid Society in Bevan's home town, and this humble organisation became the blueprint for the National Health Service. Bevan campaigned tirelessly for a medical system that would be available to everyone, free at the point of need, regardless of wealth. Despite heavy opposition, the National Health Service Act was passed in 1946, and 2,500 hospitals were nationalised in 1948, providing healthcare for the British people ever since.

Bevan continued to work as a politician until his death in 1960 at the age of sixty-two. His ashes were scattered in the hills above Tredegar, where he walked as a child. In 1972, the Bevan Memorial Stones were unveiled: the largest represents Bevan and the other three signify each constituency – Tredegar, Ebbw Vale and Rhymney. They are a lasting tribute to one of the founding fathers of the welfare state in the UK.

QUESTIONS

■ Easy

1. How many wind turbine symbols are there on the map?

2. Draw a straight line between the two golf courses on the map. What is the sum of the B-road that you traverse and the two elevations that you pass by?

■ Medium

3. The name of which cwm on the map becomes the name of another nearby cwm if an 'S' is added in the middle of its name?

4. Travelling by A-roads only, what is the minimum number of roundabouts you must traverse to get from Pochin Houses to Garden City?

■ Tricky

5. Travel as the crow flies from the capital of Guyana to a place one letter away from the capital of the Bahamas. What currency is contained in a place you travel over?

6. Where might the man who marched 10,000 men up and down a hill live?

■ Challenging

7. Starting at a Gothic Ground, go halfway towards a nice hill. Travel eastwards until you reach a National Trail. Go north and stop on the tenth diamond you pass. Travel westwards 2km. What is the only complete word in the grid square you are now in?

8. Which four places on the map are represented below? They have had their alternate letters removed.

C_U_L_Y_

F_S_I_A_ P_R_

G_Y_C_E_

T_O_D_H_W_U_C_

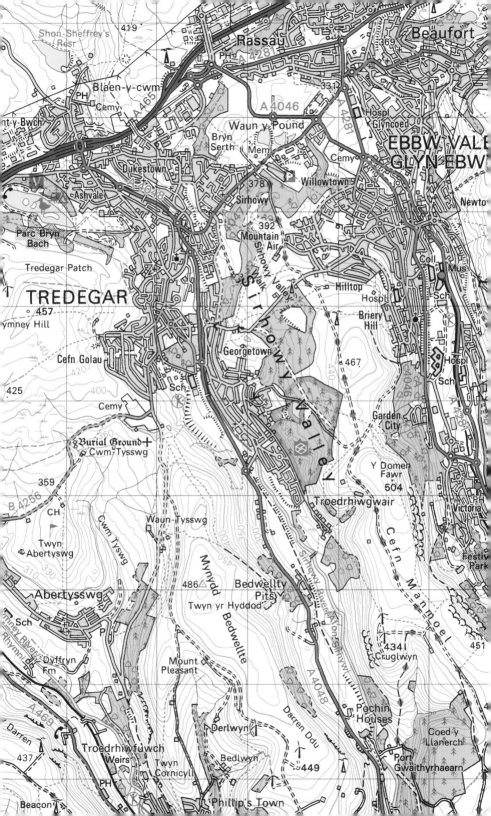

Map 17 THE EDINBURGH SEVEN

The Edinburgh Seven were the first group of women to matriculate at any British university. Sophia Jex-Blake applied to study medicine at Edinburgh University in March 1869. The faculty accepted her application, but the university deemed it inappropriate for her to attend lessons with men and too costly to set up separate classes for one woman.

Determined to become a doctor, Jex-Blake advertised in *The Scotsman* newspaper for other women who wished to study for medical qualifications. The university might consider offering a course if more women enrolled. Six responded to the advert: Isabel Thorne, Edith Pechey, Matilda Chaplin, Helen Evans, Mary Anderson and Emily Bovell. These women joined forces in November 1869 and signed the matriculation roll – they became known as the Edinburgh Seven.

Whilst more progressive circles in society supported the idea of females in the medical profession, the women faced abuse and harassment as they attended their classes. This animosity culminated in a violent riot in November 1870, at the Surgeons' Hall on Nicolson Street. The riot attracted widespread publicity and highlighted the plight of the women. Supportive students helped the women attend classes, acting as bodyguards and escorting them to and from their lectures. Many followers, including Charles Darwin, had rallied and formed a society to support the women and ensure they could complete their studies.

In 1873, a hearing at Scotland's Court of Session ruled that the women should never have been admitted to the university in the first place, and the Edinburgh Seven were legally barred from graduating and receiving their hard-earned degrees.

Jex-Blake helped establish the London School of Medicine for Women in 1874 and six of the original seven attended the school. Isabel Thorne became an honorary secretary of the school but did not pursue a career in medicine. Five of the original seven went on to study medicine abroad in Bern or Paris and receive their MDs.

New legislation in 1876 enabled examining bodies to treat men and women equally and a legal framework was established in the Universities Act of 1889 (Scotland). Edinburgh University finally admitted female undergraduates in 1892. A plaque was placed on the building in 2015 by Historic Scotland to commemorate the Surgeons' Hall Riot and the women who fought for equality in education. In 2019, Edinburgh Medical School posthumously awarded the Edinburgh Seven honorary degrees.

▇ Easy

1. Which street shares its name with a British city, and which street and place shares its name with a different British city if you add an 'L' to the end of it?

2. What is the highest measured elevation on the map? (Note, elevations on this map are in feet.)

▇ Medium

3. Where might you offer to do some woodworking?

4. What is the highest number on the map?

▇ Tricky

5. Which three letters of the alphabet do not appear on the map at all?

6. How many marked elevation points start with 'B.M.'?

▇ Challenging

7. What is the sum of the number of properties that face on to George Square and the number of tree symbols within George Square itself?

8. At the intersection of Jurassic Park's creator and Mister Darwin, head northwards and take the second left. Follow straight ahead until a waxworker and seller meet. Turn right, then turn right again at the end of this street, going through the alley to the main road. Go towards the rising sun 70 metres. Where have you arrived at?

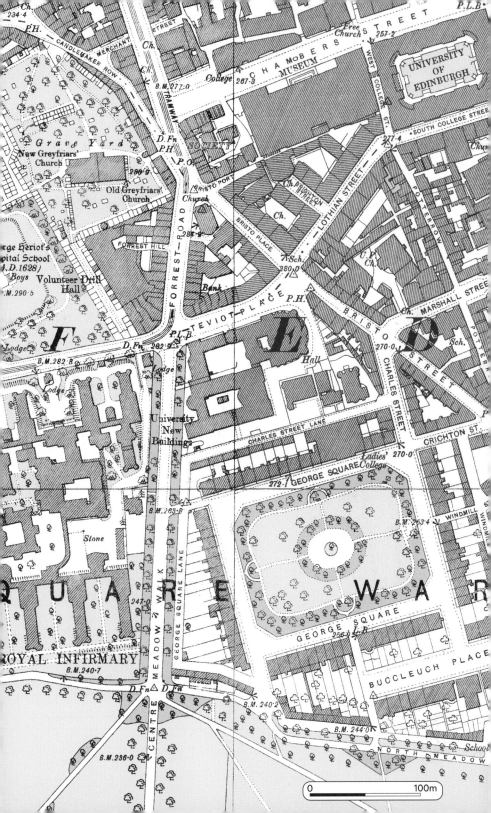

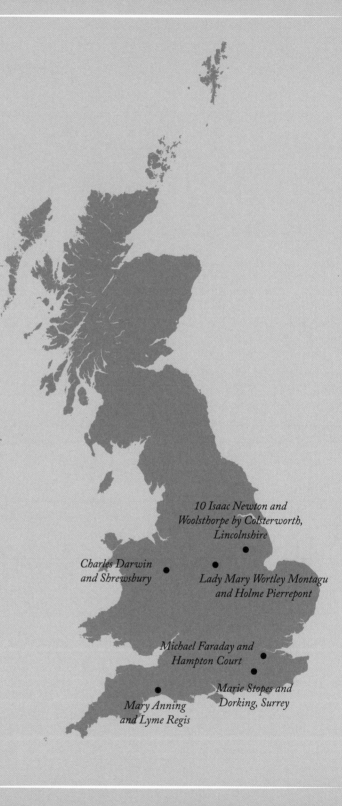

10 Isaac Newton and
Woolsthorpe by Colsterworth,
Lincolnshire

Charles Darwin
and Shrewsbury

Lady Mary Wortley Montagu
and Holme Pierrepont

Michael Faraday and
Hampton Court

Marie Stopes and
Dorking, Surrey

Mary Anning
and Lyme Regis

SCIENCE
MAKERS

18. *Isaac Newton*

———

19. *Mary Wortley Montagu*

———

20. *Michael Faraday*

———

21. *Mary Anning*

———

22. *Charles Darwin*

———

23. *Marie Stopes*

Map 18 ISAAC NEWTON AND WOOLSTHORPE BY COLSTERWORTH, LINCOLNSHIRE

Sir Isaac Newton was a mathematician, physicist and astronomer, known for his groundbreaking laws of motion and the law of universal gravitation. He is widely regarded as one of the most influential scientists in history.

Newton was born in Woolsthorpe Manor, Lincolnshire, on Christmas Day, 25 December 1642, according to the Julian calendar used in England at that time. Some historians note his birthdate as 4 January 1643, in line with the modern Gregorian calendar.

Newton came from a farming background. Sadly, his father died shortly before he was born, and his widowed mother later remarried. Young Isaac was raised by his maternal grandmother in Woolsthorpe Manor and educated at the King's School in nearby Grantham. He showed an aptitude for study and was admitted to Trinity College, Cambridge, in 1661 where he studied mathematics, physics and astronomy. In 1665, the university closed as a precaution against the Great Plague, and Newton returned to Woolsthorpe, where he continued to develop theories on optics, calculus and gravity.

In 1687, Newton published his landmark work, *Mathematical Principles of Natural Philosophy* (commonly referred to as the *Principia*) in which he described his three laws of motion, a theory that established the foundations of classical mechanics. Newton also explained his law of universal gravitation, which stated that every object in the universe attracts every other object, with a force that is proportional to their masses and inversely proportional to the square of the distance between them. This work had a profound impact on the scientific community and led to numerous advances in physics and astronomy.

Some of Newton's other notable achievements include exploring the theory of colour, the discovery of the spectrum of light and the invention of the first reflecting telescope. His development of calculus, which he called 'fluxions', laid the foundations for the type of modern mathematics that is widely used in science and engineering today.

As well as his scientific work, Newton held several high-profile positions in academia, including serving as the Lucasian Professor of Mathematics. He staunchly opposed King James II's attempt to make the universities Catholic institutions and was elected Member of Parliament for the University of Cambridge in 1689, then again in 1701.

Newton received a knighthood from Queen Anne in 1705, and he served as President of the Royal Society from 1703 until his death in 1727.

QUESTIONS

■ Easy

1. How much altitude does Planting Road gain from Easton to the B6403?

2. What place on the map might pair up with Finders Chalet?

■ Medium

3. Which contour label appears the most often?

4. Which ancient thoroughfare has its winter coat on?

■ Tricky

5. To the nearest 50m, how long is Easton Lane from the A1 to the B6403?

6. Which location on the map could cryptically mean 'mint sauce'?

■ Challenging

7. Connect a place to stay completely surrounded by the A151 to a rhyming high factory. Also connect a place for otters and molluscs to a plantation sharing its name with Kris Kardashian's maiden name.

   What's healthy in the middle?

8. The following phrases are anagrams of which places on the map?

   GOTH OTTER

   LOST ORPHANS

   SIR LANCELOT PANTING

   SECOND-RATE TOOLS

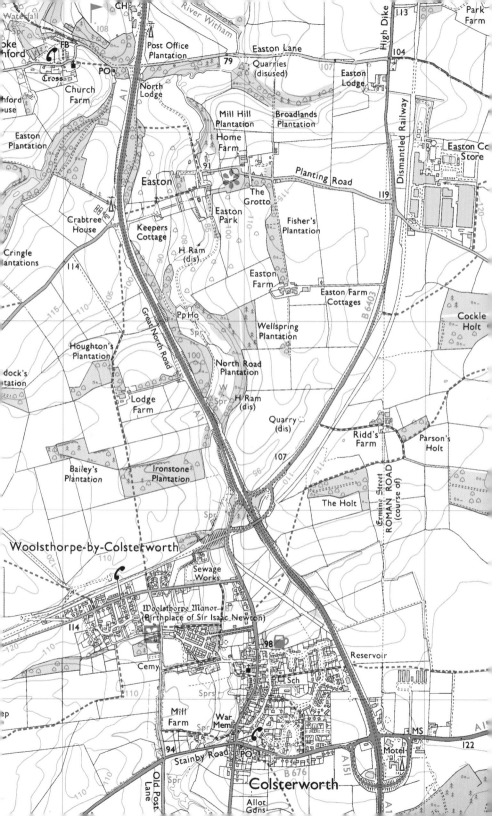

Map 19 LADY MARY WORTLEY MONTAGU AND HOLME PIERREPONT

Mary Pierrepont was born on 15 May 1689, at Holme Pierrepont Hall, the family home in Nottinghamshire. After the death of her mother and grandmother, Mary was so poorly educated by her governess that she supplemented her learning in the family library. She taught herself Latin from a book and showed an early aptitude for writing.

In 1712, she ran away and married Edward Wortley Montagu, much to her father's disapproval and after a courtship of secret correspondence. They had a son the following year and moved to London, where Edward took a position in the Treasury. Mary's wit and charm made her popular in the court of George I.

Edward was posted as ambassador to Constantinople and in 1716, Lady Mary joined him. They spent almost two years living in Turkey, during which time Mary gave birth to a daughter. Mary wrote extensively about her experiences in the Ottoman Empire, especially the warmth and generosity of the women that she encountered in the harem. The family set sail back to England through the Mediterranean, and Mary's reflections on the entire experience were documented in the *Turkish Embassy Letters* (1717)

In the early eighteenth century, smallpox was still a rife and deadly disease. Mary had lost her only brother to the illness in 1713, and her own brush with it had marked her appearance. During her time in Turkey, she witnessed the process of inoculation for the first time. Deliberately infecting a person with a mild form of smallpox in order to build immunity against a more severe form of the disease.

Lady Mary had her son undergo the process in 1718, becoming one of the first advocates of inoculation in England. Her actions persuaded members of the royal family to inoculate against smallpox and the practice became widely accepted. Lady Mary Wortley Montagu defied societal norms of the time and was a trailblazing traveller and gifted writer who contributed greatly to the literary landscape of her time. She died in London on 21 August 1762.

◼ Easy

1. What is the highest altitude label present anywhere on either map?

2. On the old map, which county is getting some hair accessories?

◼ Medium

3. If you were on first-name terms, where is 'Richard James'?

4. What comes next in this sequence?

   – YLRAP   – OC   – VID   – ??

◼ Tricky

5. How many places of worship are present on the old map, and how many of those are also present on the new map?

6. How many roundabouts are marked on the new map?

◼ Challenging

7. Starting at a solar panel by a country park, travel in straight lines to the following:

   – A hall by another country park

   – An academy between a horse course and a prickly forest

   – The Firs

   – An academy at 23m altitude

   – A place to store animals belonging to comedian Mack

   How many times do you cross over railway lines still in use?

8. Which labels on the maps are the following anagrams of? One is a red herring and does not have a match to a map label, which is it?

   OLD BATON   PITCH FERNS HERE   ATTENDANT FELT LOIN RIP

   I DO MOVE CLOTHES   VEG TACO PARCEL   ROBS POOR ELK

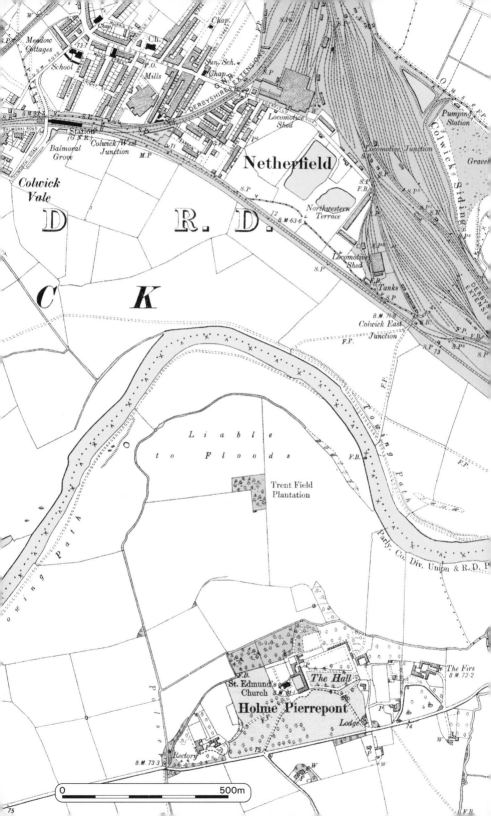

Map 20 MICHAEL FARADAY AND HAMPTON COURT

Michael Faraday was born in Newington Butts, a suburb of London, on 22 September 1791. He was from a poor family and received very little formal education. At the age of fourteen, he began working as an apprentice to a local bookbinder. During this time he began attending lectures about science at the Royal Institution of Great Britain. In 1812, he listened to talks by a chemist, Humphry Davy. Eventually, Davy recognised his talent, employing Faraday as an assistant, and pushed him to pursue his scientific interests.

Davy took an eighteen-month tour of Europe and invited Faraday along. They met many influential scientists and visited France, Italy, Switzerland and Belgium. Upon their return, Faraday assisted in experiments at the Institution, then started to conduct research of his own.

In 1831, Faraday had a breakthrough and discovered electromagnetic induction, the theory behind the modern generator. He also discovered that winding wires into coils could increase the strength of an electric current, and this led to the development of the first electric motor. All of Faraday's work transformed electricity from a magical concept into a reality that would change the world, and his work is the cornerstone of the modern electrical industry.

Faraday also made headway in the field of electrochemistry, specifically the laws of electrolysis, to do with chemical reactions and electrical currents.

He can also be credited with the discovery of the hydrocarbon benzene. The Royal Institution's Friday Evening Discourses and the Christmas Lectures are traditions that Faraday began, and both continue to this day.

Faraday accepted a role as Scientific Advisor to Trinity House from 1836 to 1865, and he remained a Professor of Chemistry at the Royal Military Academy in Woolwich from 1830 until 1851.

As a devout Christian, Faraday believed that his scientific discoveries allowed him to better understand God's creation. He never accepted any honours in his lifetime, even being offered a knighthood and a seat in Parliament. However, in 1858 he accepted official 'grace and favour' lodgings from Queen Victoria, in recognition of his contribution to science, at Hampton Court Palace. It was here that Faraday died on 25 August 1867. He is buried in Highgate Cemetery in London.

QUESTIONS

■ Easy

1. Add together the number of grid squares through which the Thames Path runs and the number of railway stations on the map. What number is the result?

2. Which sources of water are angry?

■ Medium

3. What is the sum of the numbers of the A-road and B-road labels on the map?

4. What is the first letter of the alphabet that does not appear in upper case on the map?

■ Tricky

5. Where on the map might an Inuit have once lived?

6. How many of these tree symbols are located on green backgrounds on the map?

■ Challenging

7. Starting from the place of eagles, birdies and bogeys, draw a straight line to a place that contains the name of one of Homer and Marge's children. Which of the following would you not encounter on this line:

 – Regal cat sounds

 – Something dedicated to a confused naiad

 – Sweeping tufts

 – Shoemaker's Way

8. Match up these word fragments to form the names of five places on the map:

ANT / ATI / BUS / ELD / HAM / HER / HYH / ICK / KFI / LPL / NW / ON / OND / ONP / OUSE / OVA / PAR / PTO

Map 21 MARY ANNING AND LYME REGIS

A pioneering fossil hunter and palaeontologist, Mary Anning was born in Lyme Regis in Dorset in 1799. As a small child, she collected fossils with her father along the cliffs near their home on the seafront. When a woman offered a considerable amount of money for a piece she'd found, their hobby became a profitable pastime. When Mary was only eleven years old, her father died, and her fossil hunting became an invaluable source of income to supplement her family.

At the age of twelve, Anning discovered the first complete ichthyosaurus fossil with her brother Joseph. Consequently, she became quite famous and went on to find many other important specimens.

This was not an easy time for female scientists, but Anning continued to contribute to the field of palaeontology, making multiple discoveries of prehistoric life forms along the Jurassic marine fossil bed. Male members of the scientific community would often buy specimens that she had found, cleaned and identified, but not credit Anning with any of her discoveries.

In 1828, she uncovered the remains of a pterosaur, the first discovered outside Germany. This winged creature was later named pterodactyl. Anning shared her knowledge with other scientists, including Charles Lyell, who acknowledged her contributions in his influential geological work, *Principles of Geology* (1830).

Anning died of breast cancer at the age of forty-seven. Although she was not widely recognised for her achievements in her own lifetime, she is now considered a pioneer for women in science and a trailblazer that paved the way for future palaeontologists. The Lyme Regis Museum is located on the site of her birthplace on the seafront. In 2022 a statue by sculptor Denise Dutton was unveiled depicting Anning striding towards Church Cliff with a basket and hammer and her small dog, Tray, running beside her.

QUESTIONS

◼ Easy

1. Which three places are no longer working on the old map?

2. Which place on the coast might describe the murder of Abel?

◼ Medium

3. Though I'm actually in Lancashire, my corner is on this map. What am I?

4. If you were to travel in a straight line from the top of Raymond's Hill to Wootton Cross, how many times would you pass over water?

◼ Tricky

5. What separates Amman's country from a city whose walls were destroyed in the Bible?

6. What comes next in this sequence?

   – An early coal mine alerter

   – Wide; something slightly smaller than an A-road?

   – Lengthy; pine for

   – ??

◼ Challenging

7. Starting at dove house made of timber, take a royal route, turning left when you hit a yellow road. Turn left when both the numbers 35 and 143 are important. Take the third exit where green, red and yellow all meet. Go past a plant up high. Who owns the next hill?

8. Which locations on the maps are represented by these cryptic clues?

   – M-mound

   – Newcastle set on Thor cruelly in town

   – A place for sausages to stay

   – A place that must be cleaned regularly for healthy garden aquatic life

   – Club by small bloodsucker's forest

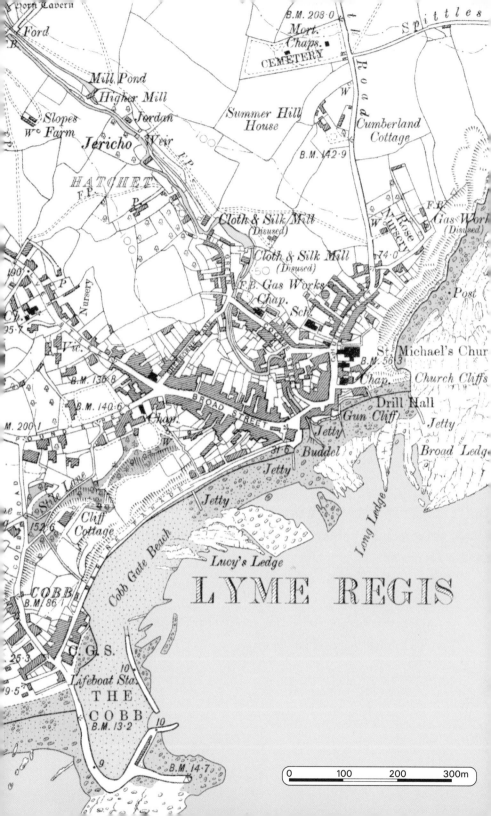

LYME BAY

Map 22 CHARLES DARWIN AND SHREWSBURY

Charles Robert Darwin revolutionised our understanding of the natural world with his theory of evolution. He was born in Shrewsbury on 12 February 1809 at The Mount, an impressive Georgian house that was built by his father Robert Darwin, a very successful local doctor.

Darwin was expected to go into medicine or become a clergyman. He attended university but neglected his studies, spending his time learning about the classification of plants, the art of taxidermy and collecting beetles.

At the age of twenty-two, he set off on the *Beagle* expedition to chart the coastline of South America. The voyage lasted five years and provided him with a lifetime of research and experience. Back in England, Darwin began collaborating with other scientists, cataloguing the findings from his voyage. He published his diaries from the trip in 1839 and became a rising star in the scientific circles of London.

Darwin continued to consider the more difficult questions about the world, and he developed his theory of natural selection. As it went against the traditionally accepted religious ideas about creation, Darwin knew his idea would be highly controversial. Eventually, in 1859 he published his famous book, *On the Origin of Species by Means of Natural Selection*, one of his most profound contributions to science.

Darwin's health had suffered but he continued to lead quite a life, performing experiments in the garden, breeding fancy pigeons and studying the flight of bumblebees. Charles Darwin died in London on 18 April 1882 and was buried in Westminster Abbey as a national hero. Darwin's theory has been scrutinised over the years, but his ideas still form the basis of how we understand the development of the natural world today.

QUESTIONS

Easy

1. Why does the old map's ferry no longer operate?

2. Where might you find a device to secure a store?

Medium

3. At what altitude, in metres or feet, is the middle of the western Water Lane?

4. Which street becomes split in two going from the old map to the new map, with both parts retaining the same name?

Tricky

5. a – I can go before Road, Avenue and Close. What am I?

   b – I can go before Road, Drive and Gardens. What am I?

   c – I can go before Street, Hill and Bank. What am I?

6. What comes next in this sequence?

   – *The Wire* actor Dominic

   – Situated in the centre of two extremes

   – Related to farming

   – ??

Challenging

7. Start at a gateway to Athens and proceed, in a straight line each time, to: An opening for Henry VIII, a stinging street, a street to quench your thirst, a verdant prominence, Irvine's arch, and finally go to The Dingle. What number have you traced out?

8. Which places on the maps share the same consonants in the same order as the clues below? (For example, the phrase 'AS I HIRE A EWE, SO I BRAY' shares the same consonants in the same order as SHREWSBURY)

   TEA IN ONE AREA, AYE

   TWO NEW ALLIES

   MINUTE CAT TAG

   SAUNA DEPOT

   ICE UP THE IRON CAR SET

Map 23 MARIE STOPES AND DORKING, SURREY

Born in Edinburgh on 15 October 1880, Marie Charlotte Carmichael Stopes was an advocate of sex education and a pioneer for birth control in Britain. Stopes started her scientific career by studying botany and geology and became a renowned palaeobotanist, obtaining a PhD specialising in fossilised plants.

In 1918, Stopes wrote an extremely controversial book, *Married Love: A New Contribution to the Solution of Sex Difficulties*. The book described the sexual side of marriage, and it was one of the first publications to discuss contraception in an accessible way. There were several reprints, and its popularity launched Stopes into the public eye.

Later in the same year, she married Humphrey Verdon Roe, the philanthropist who financed her book. The couple founded the first birth control clinic in London in 1921. It was open to all married women and offered a range of contraceptive devices to help women avoid unwanted pregnancies. Over time, many Marie Stopes clinics were opened across Britain. Further books and pamphlets were published and distributed to reach the poor and working classes. Whilst this information no doubt helped many women avoid the exhaustion of excessive childbearing, Stopes had very strong ideas regarding eugenics. At one point she campaigned for Parliament to impose compulsory sterilisation for those considered unfit for parenthood.

Stopes's strong beliefs in eugenics tainted her relationship with her son Harry, as she tried to convince him not to marry his fiancée, Mary Eyre Wallis, in case her near-sightedness was passed on to any grandchildren. He married anyway, and Stopes effectively disinherited Harry. When she died of breast cancer on 2 October 1958 at the age of seventy-seven, she left her son a dictionary and some minor effects. The Marie Stopes clinics were left to the Eugenics Society, and the rest of her estate was left to the Royal Society of Literature.

In 1938, Stopes moved to Norbury Park House, between Dorking and Leatherhead, where she spent the last twenty years of her life. The privately owned Georgian manor house was built in 1774, but a fire destroyed much of the roof and the interior of the three-storey building in March 2005. The house and its private grounds lie within Norbury Park, bought by Surrey County Council in 1931 to protect it from development. The 531-hectare parkland is run by Surrey Wildlife Trust and is open to the public.

QUESTIONS

■ Easy

1. What is the highest contour labelled on the map?

2. Which are closer together – the two stations on the east–west train line, or the two roundabouts closest to each other on the A24?

■ Medium

3. How many car parks are indicated on the map?

4. Which London Underground station on the Circle and District lines is mentioned on the map?

■ Tricky

5. What connects the following?

   – To inter

   – To spar

   – A plant part

   – A flower that 'by any other name would smell as sweet' according to Shakespeare

6. What number completes this sequence?

   226, 172, 143, 142, 122, ??

■ Challenging

7. Start in a grid square where a berry commonly used to make gin is mentioned just once. Travel west one grid square and south one grid square. Find a label made of a letter and a number. Go that compass direction that number of grid squares. If the abbreviation for farm (Fm) appears in this grid square, go south five grid squares; if not, go south three grid squares. Take the road going west, turning right just after 1km and then left at the next available junction, and travel 1km more. Where have you ended up?

8. Which locations on the map are anagrams of the following clues?

   DEVOUR DISC   BRIEFEST GROAN

   MONITOR CULT   MARK WORE BRANCH

   BARON RENTS OK

ICONIC FILM AND TV LOCATIONS

Calling all movie buffs! Great Britain is becoming more popular with the film and TV industry, with an increasing amount being filmed here. We have compiled a list of iconic film and TV locations. Visiting these is not only great fun, but it is also a great way to explore unseen places across the country.

SCOTLAND

Skyfall **(James Bond): Glen Etive, Glencoe.** Glen Etive is famous for being the driving route to James Bond's family home in the Scottish Highlands.

Trainspotting: **Princes Street, Edinburgh.** One of the busiest streets in Edinburgh, Princes Street is much more than a shopping destination and is famously used in the opening scene of this cult classic.

WALES

Harry Potter and the Deathly Hallows: **Freshwater West beach, Pembrokeshire National Park.** The beach was used in 2011 for filming the burial of Dobby the house elf.

The Dark Knight Rises: **Henrhyd Falls, Bannau Brycheiniog (Brecon Beacons).** Close to cooling lakes and running waterfalls, this is the perfect place to spend a hot summer's day. It was also used as the entrance to the iconic Batcave.

EAST ENGLAND

Dad's Army: **Thetford, Norfolk.** If you are a fan of the sitcom filmed in the 1960s and 70s you will want to stop here for a visit. Thetford Guildhall was used as the fictional Walmington-on-Sea town hall.

LONDON

Notting Hill: **Notting Hill district.** One of the most famous films from the 1990s, featuring Hugh Grant and Julia Roberts. The blue door behind which Hugh Grant's character lived can be found at 280 Westbourne Park Road.

Love Actually: **Selfridges department store.** Walk the aisles and remember the iconic scene of Alan Rickman trying to buy a present in secret from Rowan Atkinson.

NORTHEAST

Harry Potter and the Philosopher's Stone/Chamber of Secrets: **Alnwick Castle, Northumberland.** The castle was used as the magical Hogwarts School of Witchcraft and Wizardry in the first two films.

Robin Hood: Prince of Thieves: **Sycamore Gap, Northumberland.** Sycamore Gap is the location of a sycamore tree sitting in front of Hadrian's Wall. The site is famous for being used in the Kevin Costner film and the tree is one of the most photographed in the country.

NORTHWEST

Miss Potter: **Derwentwater, Keswick, Lake District.** The Lakes was once home to Beatrix Potter, author of many bestselling children's books, and in 2006 her story came to life here in film.

Peaky Blinders: **Northern Quarter, Greater Manchester.** The Northern Quarter has an industrial feel and has become famous for featuring in the cult BBC series. The most prominent filming locations have been the NQ's Dale Street, Mangle Street and Back Piccadilly.

SOUTH

His Dark Materials: Oxford University, Oxfordshire. The BBC TV series is based on the trilogy of novels by Philip Pullman. It first aired in November 2019 and the third and final series aired in 2022.

Dunkirk: Dorset and Hampshire. In Christopher Nolan's retelling of Dunkirk, several locations in Dorset and Hampshire were used. From port scenes showing the preparation of the boats to various railways, these counties offer an assortment of sites.

SOUTHWEST

Alice in Wonderland: Antony House, Cornwall. Cornwall is a paradise all year round due to its sandy beaches and old cobbled towns. Visited by people from across the world, the county also appears in Tim Burton's version of this classic children's book.

Die Another Day (James Bond): Eden Project, Cornwall. The Eden Project was used as 007 enemy Gustav Graves' Icelandic palace. The interior biodome of the film was filmed here.

Star Wars: The Force Awakens: Puzzlewood, Forest of Dean. Puzzlewood is a magical 14-acre ancient woodland site located close to the market town of Coleford. Many movies and TV shows including *Doctor Who* and *Merlin* have been filmed here. It was also used for *The Force Awakens* in scenes featuring Han Solo, Chewie, Rey and Maz Kanata.

YORKSHIRE & HUMBER

Downton Abbey: North York Moors Railway, North Yorkshire. The historical drama has featured lots of locations from around North Yorkshire. The most famous is the North York Moors Railway, which was used in the opening scene. Pickering railway station was also used as a stand-in for King's Cross (London).

Enjoy exploring these film locations across Great Britain!

Glen Etive,
Glencoe

Princes Street,
Edinburgh

Alnwick Castle,
Northumberland

Sycamore Gap,
Northumberland

North York Moors Railway,
North Yorkshire

Derwentwater,
Keswick, Lake District

Northern Quarter,
Greater Manchester

Thetford, Norfolk

Freshwater West beach,
Pembrokeshire National Park

Puzzlewood Forest,
Forest of Dean

Oxford University,
Oxfordshire

Notting Hill

Selfridges
department store

Henrhyd Falls,
Bannau Brycheiniog

Eden Project,
Cornwall

Dorset and
Hampshire

Anthony House,
Cornwall

Charles Rennie Mackintosh
and Townhead, Glasgow

Walter Scott and
Abbotsford

Beatrix Potter and
Near Sawrey, Cumbria

Emily Brontë
and Thornton

William Shakespeare and
Stratford-upon-Avon

JMW Turner and
Covent Garden

Thomas Hardy
and Dorchester

Agatha Christie and
Greenway, Galmpton

ARTISTIC
CREATORS

24. *William Shakespeare*

25. *Sir Walter Scott*

26. *JMW Turner*

27. *Emily Brontë*

28. *Thomas Hardy*

29. *Beatrix Potter*

30. *Charles Rennie Mackintosh*

31. *Agatha Christie*

Map 24 WILLIAM SHAKESPEARE AND STRATFORD-UPON-AVON

Known simply as 'The Bard' and widely regarded as the greatest writer in history, William Shakespeare was a playwright, a poet and an actor. He was born in Stratford-upon-Avon, Warwickshire in 1564. The son of John Shakespeare, a glove maker, and Mary Arden, the daughter of a wealthy landowner, Shakespeare attended the local Grammar School and studied Latin, Greek and classical literature. Aged eighteen, he married Anne Hathaway, who was pregnant with their first child, Susanna. They went on to have twins, Hamnet and Judith, but sadly, Hamnet died at the age of eleven.

By 1592, Shakespeare had established himself as a successful playwright. His plays included comedies such as *The Taming of the Shrew* (1590) and tragedies like *Romeo and Juliet* (1595), *King Lear* (1605) and *Hamlet* (1600). In all, Shakespeare wrote at least thirty-seven plays and over 150 sonnets.

From 1599, Shakespeare had a share in the Globe Theatre, giving him a place to stage his works to members of the public. People from all walks of life attended, from lords and ladies to the working-class 'groundlings' who watched from the dirt floor in front of the stage.

William Shakespeare died on 23 April 1616, at the age of fifty-two. He was buried in the chancel of the Holy Trinity Church in Stratford. Shakespeare had a profound impact on literature and the development of the English language, contributing around 1,700 words and phrases that are still used today. His work is celebrated around the world for its insight into the human condition as well as its dramatic power, wit and wisdom.

Stratford-upon-Avon is a town dedicated to Shakespeare, and there are numerous tributes and memorials to commemorate his work. The cottage where he was born, Anne Hathaway's cottage, and Shakespeare's New Place are open to the public and form part of Shakespeare's Birthplace Trust, to protect and promote his legacy.

■ Easy

1. Which village becomes a hazard from a thunderstorm if an H is added to its beginning?

2. You are standing at the viewpoint at Welcombe Hills Country Park, looking towards Stratford-upon-Avon. Which of these, as you look at them, is furthest on your left?

   – Anne Hathaway's Cottage   – Racecourse

   – Clopton Bridge   – Mason Croft

■ Medium

3. What adornment does Holy Trinity Church have; a tower or a spire/ minaret/dome?

4. What features are located 500m WNW and 750m ESE of Ingon?

■ Tricky

5. W: Cambridgeshire cathedral city

   N: Elevated

   E: Ovine creatures

   S: ?

6. At what altitude is the hill on the map next to a place that shares its name with the title of a novel by Stella Gibbons?

■ Challenging

7. What comes next?

   340046, 4394086, 4223400, ?

8. Which labels on the maps are represented by these clues which have had their alternate letters removed?

   _U_L _T_E_T   _N_ E_M _R_D_E

   _I_D_N_T_N   _U_Y'_ L_C_S

   _O_L_W _E_D_W

   _O_P_L _A_

   _A_W_C_ R_A_ N_R_E_Y

e Elm
Bridge

B.M. 146·3

B.M. 145·1

B.M. 12

St. Greg
R. C. C

ST. GREGORY'S ROAD

139·8

Lock

Warwick Road
Nursery

M.P Warwick 8
B.M. 126·9

B.M. 132·3

Lock

SHAKESPEARE STREET

MULBERRY ST.

GREAT WILLIAM STREET

TYLER ST.

JOHN ST.

PAYTON STREET

Ch.

Chap.

Chap.

Chap.

B.M. 120·5

WARWICK ROAD

P

GUILD STREET

HENLEY STREET

WINDSOR STREET

Sch.

MEER ST.

UNION STREET

Sm.y.

P.H.

Memorial
Fn.

WOOD STREET

135·9 BRIDGE ST.

BRIDGE FOOT

CATTLE
MARKET

130·6

STREET

HIGH STREET

SHEEP STREET

BASIN

F.B.

ELY STREET

CHAPEL ST.

Wharf

WATERSIDE

THE
BANCROFT

Clopton
Bridge

SCHOLARS LANE

CHURCH STREET

CHAPEL LANE

Avon

126·1

Boat Ho.

124·8

Boat
Houses

119·8

Mason
Croft

Inn

122

Shakespeare
Memorial Theatre

River

131·4

128·2

SOUTHERN LANE

Ferry

Cricket
Ground

Pavilion

STRATFORD ON AVON & LONGDON ROAD TRAMWAY
(Disused)

G. W. R.

BULL STREET

Avon Bank

Recreation
Ground

College
(Site of)

COLLEGE STREET

TOWN

0   100   200m

RYLANDS

COLLEGE LANE

126·7

Holy Trinity
Church

125·8

Lucy's Locks

Eastwell
House

Map 25 SIR WALTER SCOTT AND ABBOTSFORD

Born in Edinburgh in 1771, Walter Scott was an intelligent child. He was sent to university at the age of twelve but left at fourteen to work in his father's office as an apprentice. As Sheriff-Depute of Selkirkshire, Scott spent time travelling through small villages and towns. People exchanged their stories for money, and Scott shaped them into his first book, *Minstrelsy of the Scottish Border*, in 1802. He gained instant fame for his ability to deliver a riveting plot, producing several narrative poems over the next decade.

Scott wrote his first novel *Waverley* in 1814 but published it anonymously. The book was immensely popular and led to over two dozen additional 'Waverley Novels' that included *Rob Roy* (1817) and *Ivanhoe* (1819). Before his work became prevalent, little was known about Scotland, and his novels played a central part in defining a national identity.

By the age of forty, Scott was world-famous as a writer, but he continued to work as a lawyer. He wanted to build a country home for his French wife Charlotte and their children and bought land near the small town of Melrose. Scott built Abbotsford, a country house befitting a man of his importance. This stately home became his driving force, where he wrote to fund the acquisition of land and possessions.

Sir Walter Scott's impressive collection of ephemera can still be seen in Abbotsford and includes: a lock of Bonnie Prince Charlie's hair, Rob Roy's purse and even a scrap of dress material from Mary Queen of Scots.

Accumulating this collection was not a cheap hobby, and in 1825, a banking crisis forced Scott to face financial ruin. Given his status, he was offered ways out of the debt, but Scott decided to dedicate himself to writing and earning enough to pay his creditors. He managed to write prolifically, despite the tragic loss of his wife Charlotte in 1826. Scott's health suffered and he eventually died of a stroke at the age of sixty-one.

■ Easy

1. Which hill might have a party?

2. The old buildings of Brunswickhill, Netherby and Abbotshill are located on which current-day road?

■ Medium

3. What feature has both a 600ft contour and a 200m contour running through it on the historical and modern maps respectively?

4. Which location becomes the name of an Oscar-winning director if the first letter is removed and a space added?

■ Tricky

5. What comes next in this sequence?

   – A stringed musical instrument with strings of multiple colours

   – Deer's dwelling

   – Spongy flowerless plant's cottage

   – ??

6. To the nearest 100m, how far is it from the Post Office to the museum?

■ Challenging

7. Start at the point where the Southern Upland and Borders Abbeys Ways meet. Proceed directly to what sounds like actor Close's grassland. Go straight to where someone tending a flock might stay, and then draw a straight line to a point at an altitude of 234m. Go as the crow flies to a roundabout where an A- and a B- road meet with numbers that differ by 269. Take the A-road northwest, stopping at the next roundabout you come to. What letter have you drawn out?

8. Which labels on the maps are represented by the following clues that have had their vowels removed and consonants respaced?

   GNK NW LCH

   NW FN

   BBT SM SS

   NG LS HMN SSK

   PP RFL DN SD

COTTAGE
HOSPITAL

M.S

B.M. 439·3

Galashiels 1
Selkirk 5

By.

P

Abbotshill

452

Newhaan

Netherby

B.M. 441·2

runswickhill

W

Netherbarns

428

400

B.M. 418·5

Lodges

24

M.P.

The Hawthorns

S.P.

Glenmain Pool

River Tweed

Harp Pool

Gravel Pit

Under
Thicket

Upper Thicket

Gas Works

S.P

S.P

400

Lodge

Nether Place

Kingsknowes
M.P.

Abbot's
(Disused

400

Lynhurst

400

S.P *Deadwater Pool*

N.B.R.
SELKIRK BRANCH

Ferry

Mosshouse Pool

Newhart Haugh

Abbotsford

Hindshouse Pool

Ford

Lodge

P

W.

Reservoir

500

Well

600

Roman Po

0			300m

Map 26 JMW TURNER AND COVENT GARDEN

Joseph Mallord William Turner was born above his father William's barber shop in 1775. The man hailed as 'The Father of Modern Art' came from fairly modest beginnings. His father had relocated from Devon and his mother, Mary Marshall, was from a long line of prosperous local butchers and shopkeepers. The house at 21 Maiden Lane no longer exists, but a plaque marks the spot where William Turner carried out his trade as a hairdresser and wigmaker and his young son exhibited his first works of art on the walls of the shop.

At the age of fourteen, Turner was enrolled in the Royal Academy of Arts and held his first exhibition at fifteen. An interest in architecture made him a master of perspective and he became a Royal Academy Professor on the subject in 1807, where he taught until 1828.

Despite growing up in the shadowy backstreets of Covent Garden, Turner's immense talent lay in his ability to portray light and intense seascapes. He was a prolific artist, and over the course of his life he produced over 30,000 sketches, 550 oil paintings and around 2,000 watercolours. Turner is one of those rare historical artists who managed to find fortune and fame in his lifetime. His work is displayed in Tate Britain, with some key pieces held by the National Gallery.

Turner's Covent Garden has changed over the past two centuries. The Market Hall was constructed in 1830 to provide a more permanent trading centre. One of the most famous eighteenth-century coffee houses, Button's, was located at 10 Russell Street. Members of the public were invited to submit material for possible publication in *The Guardian* newspaper, posting it through a marble letter box in the shape of a lion's head. The letter box was acquired over a century ago by the Duke of Bedford for display in his ancestral home, Woburn Abbey.

In the heart of Covent Garden stands St Paul's Church, where Turner's parents were married, Turner was baptised and his father was laid to rest. St Paul's is known as 'the Actors' Church' and contains many tributes to members of the theatrical profession. Turner placed a memorial plaque to his parents here in 1832.

JMW Turner was considered an eccentric man; he never married and suffered severe bouts of depression. He died of cholera in December 1851 and is buried in St Paul's Cathedral.

QUESTIONS

◾ Easy

1. How many symbols for places of worship are there on the map?

2. Which London Underground station is located at a junction of two roads, one of which has a number 105 times the other?

◾ Medium

3. Which royal can be found just to the south of the building with this shape?

4. To the nearest 50m, how far apart are Denmark and Portugal at their closest points?

◾ Tricky

5. Where on the map might the CIA be located?

6. Start on a flowery street where it meets with a gesture of respect. Head towards some wet-weather footwear, but turn left when you reach Crowe's road. Head northwest at the lane, and turn right on to a pen maker's street. Turn right where Charles III might move back and forth. Take the second right. What letter might make your current location a tiger?

◾ Challenging

7. How many British cities are mentioned on the map? (If a city is mentioned more than once, just count it once.)

8. Which labels on the map are represented below by the alternate letter clues?

_H_ M_L_

_I_G_ C_L_E_E

_R_T_S_ M_S_U_

_I_T_R_A _M_A_K_E_T

_E_ L_O_ S_U_R_

_E_T_V_L _I_R

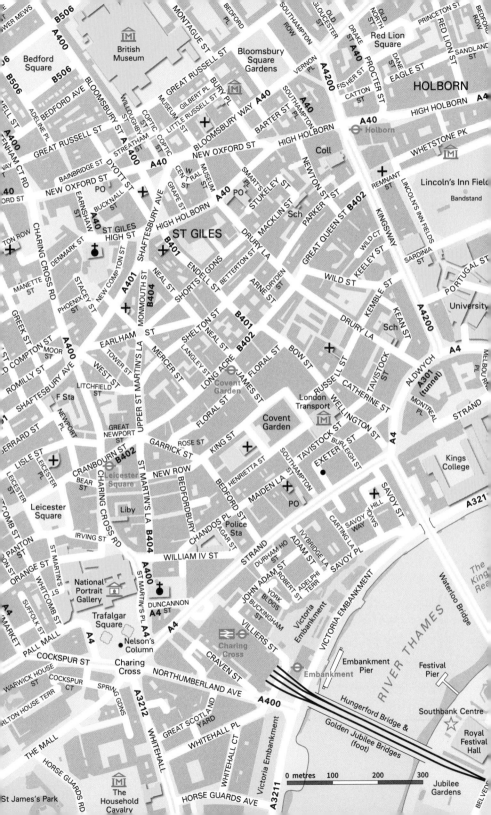

Map 27 EMILY BRONTË AND THORNTON

Born in the village of Thornton on 30 July 1818, Emily Jane Brontë was the fifth of six children. In 1821, the Brontë family moved into the parsonage at Haworth. Emily's mother died of cancer later that year, and her Aunt Branwell arrived to look after the family.

At the age of six, Emily and her older sisters were sent to school in Lancashire. Maria and Elizabeth became seriously ill and died of tuberculosis within weeks of each other. Emily and her older sister Charlotte returned to Haworth to be educated at home, having free access to any books in their father's library. Charlotte, Emily, Anne and their brother Branwell became extremely close. They played on the expanse of wild moor that surrounded their home and didn't socialise with other children. They all read extensively and made up stories of imaginary lands, inspired by a set of toy soldiers given to Branwell.

The three sisters planned to open a school of their own, but Emily only ever worked as a teacher for six months in 1838, at Law Hill School near Halifax. The job proved to be quite a strain on her fragile health. In 1842, she accompanied Charlotte to Brussels, where they attended an academy to perfect their French and German, but the two returned to Haworth when their aunt died. In 1844, they tried to open a school in their home, but the remote location made this untenable.

Fearing sexism and prejudice, the three sisters published their collected works in 1846, *Poems by Currer, Ellis and Acton Bell*, using male pseudonyms. The book only sold two copies. The following year Emily published her novel *Wuthering Heights* under the name Ellis Bell.

In September of 1848, Branwell Brontë died suddenly, and Emily caught a chill attending his funeral. Her illness developed into inflammation of the lungs, then tuberculosis. Emily died on the sofa in the dining room on 19 December 1848, at the age of thirty.

The area known as 'Brontë Country' lies between Manchester and Leeds, covering an expanse of West Yorkshire and East Lancashire. Thornton is west of the city of Bradford, with a population of around 17,000. A blue plaque commemorates the birthplace of Emily and her famous siblings at 74 Market Street. The family home in Haworth is now the Brontë Parsonage Museum.

QUESTIONS

■ Easy

1. North of Brontë Way (marked by green diamonds), three public houses form a triangle. Which area lends its name to a road in that area?

2. How many becks are labelled on the map?

■ Medium

3. Take the name of a famous cricketing almanac and insert an 'L' somewhere in it. This shares its name with a B-road with what number?

4. Which hill on the map sounds like it should be 'desserted'?

■ Tricky

5. From Aldersley Farm, take a lengthy road until it is 304m in elevation. Turn left, keep going along a university official's path until you reach a public telephone. Return along that road, taking the first main right turn after you've passed Cairo's country. Stop at the next junction. What letter have you traced out?

6. What connects: Heads, Hill, Holland, Hole and House?

■ Challenging

7. Locate the base of the wind turbine next to the highest contour label, and the milestone nearest to a Post Office (assume the milestone is on the road immediately north of its label). How far apart are they, to the nearest 100m?

8. Which locations are anagrams of the following words or phrases?

ERODE GRAPH

'KEEP UP', I REPLY

LEGO CHAFED BULLY

PILATES

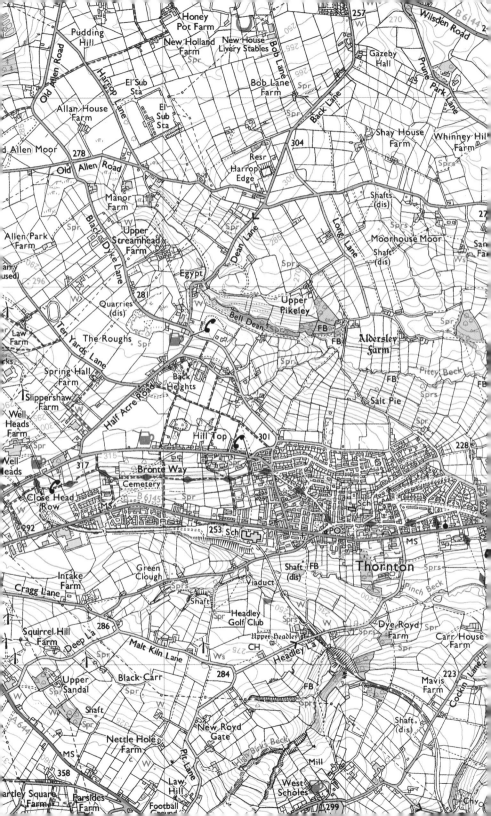

Map 28 THOMAS HARDY AND DORCHESTER

Thomas Hardy was an English novelist and poet, known for his portrayals of rural life in Victorian England. He was born on 2 June 1840 in the small village of Higher Bockhampton, near Dorchester, and was the eldest son of a stonemason.

Hardy's mother educated him at home until the age of eight, then he received a formal education in Dorchester, at Mr Last's Academy for Young Gentlemen. Unable to afford a university education, his family arranged for an apprenticeship in architecture. Hardy enjoyed a successful career in London, and there is much evidence of his work around the city. Eventually, he returned to Dorset to work as a freelance architect, and during this time he began to write.

Whilst working in Cornwall in 1870, Hardy met Emma Gifford, and the couple eventually married in 1874. In the same year, His fourth novel, *Far From the Madding Crowd* (1874), became his breakthrough work, being both commercially successful and critically acclaimed.

Hardy went on to produce some powerful novels, including *The Mayor of Casterbridge* (1886) and *Tess of the d'Urbervilles* (1891). Most of his stories dealt with the everyday struggles of normal people and their inner conflict between desire and duty.

In 1885, the Hardys moved into Max Gate, a home that Thomas had designed himself. After the publication of *Jude the Obscure* (1895) he gave up writing novels, but he continued to write poetry. He was a prolific poet, but his first collection, *Wessex Poems,* wasn't published until 1898.

Emma died in 1912, and Hardy was bereft, despite the couple drifting apart during their marriage. To process his grief, he wrote a book of poetry, *Poems 1912–13,* in the form of an elegy, examining the couple's relationship in a very honest and direct way. In 1914, Hardy married his secretary, Florence Emily Dugdale, who was thirty-nine years younger, although she found the marriage difficult due to his continuing public adoration of Emma. Hardy developed pleurisy in December 1927 and he died at Max Gate on 11 January 1928.

Hardy's work is studied and appreciated for its rich characterisation and descriptions of the English countryside. His tragic depictions of rural life are more realistic than most other authors of the Victorian era.

A memorial statue of Hardy was erected in Dorchester in 1950. His birthplace, Hardy's Cottage, and his marital home, Max Gate, are owned by the National Trust.

QUESTIONS

■ Easy

1. True or false: All labels with blue diagonal-line shading begin with the same letter.

2. What did the Romans call Dorchester?

■ Medium

3. What is the difference between the highest and lowest contour labels on the map?

4. Which village on the map has a region of forest in the shape of a horseshoe?

■ Tricky

5. Where might you defeat a gardening cart?

6. Why might a narrator of *The War of the Worlds*, a footless ship of the desert and the capital of Jamaica all sound like they make a living on top of a mountain?

■ Challenging

7. What is the maximum number of different roundabouts you can traverse when travelling from the 65m altitude marker on the A354 by Winterborne Monkton to the A35 northeast of Stinsford? You are only allowed to travel on orange- or green-coloured roads, and you are not allowed to travel on the same part of a road twice (i.e. no doubling back on yourselves).

8. Pair up these words to form the names of six locations on the map. One word is a red herring, but which one?

BORNE / BURY / COW / DEN / DON / GATE / HARDY / HAY / HERRINGS / HILL / LEAP / POUND / TON / WAY / WINTER / WOLF

Map 29 BEATRIX POTTER AND NEAR SAWREY, CUMBRIA

Helen Beatrix Potter was one of the world's best-loved children's authors. Although she is very much associated with the Lake District, Potter was born at 2 Bolton Gardens, South Kensington, on 28 July 1866 and lived in the family home until her marriage.

Beatrix had a younger brother, Bertram, but she was educated by governesses and a series of tutors and spent a lot of time alone as a child. From a very young age, she was fascinated by nature and had a menagerie of wild animals that she would 'collect' and keep as pets in the classroom at home. Drawing these creatures and creating stories kept her amused.

One particular governess, Annie Moore, became a lifelong friend. *The Tale of Peter Rabbit* began when she wrote a letter to Annie's little boy, Noel. Potter based the titular character on her own pet, a Belgian buck rabbit named Peter Piper whom she would often walk on a lead. The original manuscript was rejected by several commercial publishers, so in 1901 Potter self-published and paid for the first print run of 250 copies. The following year the book was taken on by Frederick Warne & Co. and required six print runs due to its popularity.

In 1905, Potter purchased Hill Top Farm in the village of Near Sawrey in the Lake District. That summer, her publisher Norman Warne proposed to her, but her parents would not formally acknowledge their betrothal or allow the marriage. Warne died of leukaemia weeks after their engagement. Potter did find love later in life. In 1913 she married a local solicitor, William Heelis, and they lived in Castle Cottage in Near Sawrey. After her marriage, Potter spent more time on her farms and managing her land. One of the founders of the National Trust, Hardwicke Rawnsley, became a close friend. Upon her death in 1943, Potter left fifteen farms and four thousand acres of land to the Trust. Hill Top was opened to the public in 1946.

Near Sawrey and the neighbouring village Far Sawrey date back to the fourteenth century, on a historic trade route that ran from Kendal to Hawkshead, now the B5285 and B5284. They are thriving communities with plenty of traditional events, local produce shows and May Queen celebrations. Near Sawrey has a village pub and Far Sawrey has the parish church and the village shop.

QUESTIONS

■ Easy

1. On the map, what connects Dumbarton, Heald and Station Scar?

2. What is the sum of the numbers present in the same grid square as Sandy Nab?

■ Medium

3. On which piece of land would Disney's 'Beast' find his one true love?

4. Does the only place of worship marked on the map have a tower or a spire?

■ Tricky

5. Where on the map can you find some *Convallaria majalis*?

6. What four common bird names can be found in locations on the map?

■ Challenging

7. Starting at Moray Mansion, head to a cliff made of porridge, then go to a place where silver could be nearby. Then travel to the only bracketed number on the map, and finally go to where someone looking after Big Ben might come ashore. What letter have you traced out with this path?

8. Piece these fragments together to construct the name of four places on the map. Which one fragment is left over after this is done?

BROW / COLT / COTTAGES / CRAB / CUCKOO / HEIGHTS / HOUSE / LONG / PAR / ROCK / STONE / TREE / WOOD

Map 30 CHARLES RENNIE MACKINTOSH AND TOWNHEAD, GLASGOW

The fourth of eleven children, Charles Rennie Mackintosh was born at 70 Parson Street, Townhead, Glasgow, in 1868. He was a sickly child and doctors prescribed fresh air and holidays. His family took him on tours of the countryside during which he sketched his observations of nature and plants. At fifteen, Mackintosh first enrolled at the Glasgow School of Art, where he studied drawing, painting, modelling and design. He also had an apprenticeship in architecture. He became a partner with the architectural firm Honeyman and Keppie in 1901.

Sometime around 1892, he met Margaret Macdonald, a skilled artist in her own right. They married in 1900 and were partners in every sense of the word. Charles often reminded contemporaries of his wife's influence, once writing, 'Margaret has genius. I only have talent.' They considered architecture a supreme discipline that pulled all aspects of their art together. Their projects focused on the design as a whole and not the individual parts. They incorporated architecture, furniture, graphic design, textiles and painting, most often inspired by nature.

A change in architectural fashion and a decline in his workload led to Mackintosh moving to Walberswick in Suffolk in 1914, where he worked on watercolours, particularly flowers and landscapes. In 1923, the couple moved to Port-Vendres in southern France and Mackintosh dedicated himself to painting, but in 1927 they moved back to London. Mackintosh was diagnosed with cancer, and died on 10 December 1928. Margaret complied with his last wishes and scattered his ashes in the bay of Port-Vendres.

Mackintosh was one of the first pioneers of modern architecture and design, defining art nouveau and putting Glasgow on the artistic map. Many examples of his work remain around the city, including the Willow Tearooms on Sauchiehall Street, and others include Hill House in Helensburgh.

QUESTIONS

■ Easy

1. Who owns a building with this shape?

2. Which saint has a street on one map
   and an avenue and place on the other?

■ Medium

3. How many of the first names of The Beatles are mentioned in places on
   the maps?

4. Which location, marked on the old map but not on the new map, shares its
   name with a landmark in Venice, Cambridge, Oxford and Chester?

■ Tricky

5. Which road sounds like it has a toll on it?

6. On the new map, stand at the junction of Havannah Street and Hunter
   Street. Looking along Havannah Street, on the left-hand side are two
   buildings that look like numbers. Make this a two-digit number with the
   building furthest away from you the first digit (i.e. in the tens position).
   Multiply this number with the number of labels for public houses (marked
   as P.H. or P.Hs.) on the old map. What number is the result?

■ Challenging

7. On the newer map, start at a point where 7 points is next to 3 points. Travel
   in straight lines to financial centres in New York City, a site for Santa to
   heal, the junction of someone working with stone and someone working
   with thread, the southernmost extent of the 'mate' road, and then go
   straight to the start again. What letter does this route draw?

8. Match up these word fragments to make the names of six locations on
   the grids:

   BAR / BOW / CIR / CUS / EEN / EET / ERY / GGR / HTH / ILL / KHO / LIN / LOC /
   MET / NEC / OLI / ONY / ROP / ROT / ROW / SCE / SIG / SPI / STR / TAL / TEN

Map 31 AGATHA CHRISTIE AND GREENWAY, GALMPTON

Known worldwide as a best-selling novelist, Agatha Mary Clarissa Miller was born in Torquay on 15 September 1890. Mostly educated at home by her mother Clara, Agatha came from a wealthy, upper-middle-class family.

Agatha met Archie Christie in 1912 and they married on Christmas Eve 1914, taking their honeymoon in the Grand Hotel in Torquay. The couple had a daughter, Rosalind, but their marriage was not a happy one. In 1926, Archie asked for a divorce and Agatha disappeared for eleven days. Registered under the name of her husband's mistress, she was found safe and well in a hotel in Harrogate, but never fully explained what happened during her absence.

In 1930, Agatha met and married Max Mallowan, an archaeologist. The couple travelled to Middle Eastern archaeological digs together, and Agatha used this setting in several novels and short stories. In 1938 they bought Greenway, in Galmpton. This impressive Georgian house was a property Agatha had always admired, perched above the River Dart with spectacular views. Greenway became their holiday home, a special place to spend time with family and friends.

During World War II, Greenway was requisitioned and used to house child evacuees. It was returned to Agatha and Max on Christmas Day 1945. There was very little damage, but one American had painted a fresco in the library. When they offered to paint over the 'graffiti' Agatha told them, '. . . it would be a historic memorial, and I was delighted to have it.' Greenway was given to the National Trust in 2000, and the house contains many significant artefacts from Max's work as well as first editions of Agatha's books.

Christie wrote sixty-six detective novels featuring characters such as Miss Marple and Hercule Poirot, and fourteen short story collections. Christie also wrote the world's longest-running play, *The Mouse Trap*. Agatha Christie's books have sold over a billion in the English language and over a billion in translation, and her novels are outsold only by Shakespeare and the Holy Bible.

QUESTIONS

■ Easy

1. Who studies here?

2. What chore might you do just south of a forest for rabbit-like animals?

■ Medium

3. What are the highest labelled contours on each map, and which one is higher?

4. Where might you scare dried grass?

■ Tricky

5. To the north: 99 (379)

   To the south: 104 (3205)

   What's the highest height in the middle?

6. The word 'ton' often appears at the end of place names, meaning 'settlement' or 'town'. How many times does 'ton' appear in labels on the new map (either on its own or as part of a longer word)?

■ Challenging

7. Ferry Cottage -> Cottage Farm

   Lower Gurrow Point -> Hole

   Bozomzeal Cross -> Higher Greenway

   East Cornworthy -> Lower Greenway/Flat Owers Mud

   Thinking about just the old map, what letter have you traced out?

8. Which locations on the maps are represented by the following cryptic clues?

   House's plant protector contains passage

   Sour cream kept long in inlet

   Town's royal garb

   Dumps roughly around heated crime in boggy region

   Cove's condiment accompanies bird-swallowing cobalt and vanadium

   Settlement's endless song is a pig product

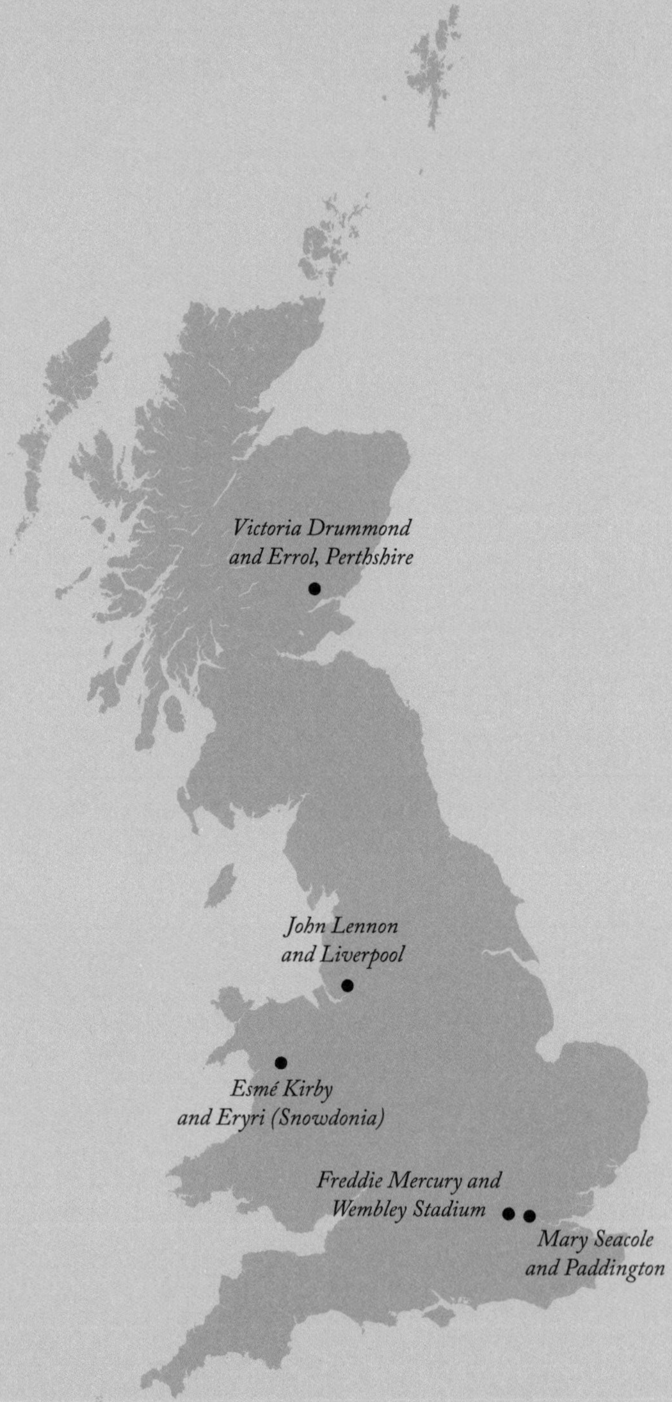

Victoria Drummond
and Errol, Perthshire
●

John Lennon
and Liverpool
●

Esmé Kirby
and Eryri (Snowdonia)
●

Freddie Mercury and
Wembley Stadium
● ●
Mary Seacole
and Paddington

SHAKERS AND MOVERS

32. *Mary Seacole*

33. *Victoria Drummond*

34. *Esmé Kirby*

35. *John Lennon*

36. *Freddie Mercury*

Map 32 MARY SEACOLE AND PADDINGTON

Born Mary Jane Grant in Kingston, Jamaica, in 1805, her father was a Scottish army officer and her mother ran a boarding house, Blundell Hall. Mrs Grant was also known as 'The Doctress', a respected healer who used traditional Jamaican herbs as medicine. Young Mary carefully observed her mother's methods and practised her healing skills on her dolls.

In 1836, Mary married Edwin Seacole, but was widowed eight years later. She travelled to Cruces in Panama to visit her brother in 1850, but during her stay, there was a virulent outbreak of cholera. Seacole treated the sick with rubs and poultices, which saved countless lives. When she returned to Jamaica, she was put in charge of the training of nurses in the British military camp. It was here that she first heard horrific stories about the Crimean War.

Seacole was compelled to help wounded soldiers on the battlefront, so she travelled to England to volunteer her services. First, she requested a meeting with the Secretary of State for War, but he refused to see her. She then applied to Florence Nightingale, who had advertised for nurses and helpers in the national newspapers. Her application was rejected. With the financial help of friends, Seacole organised a medical unit and 'The British Hotel' was established close to the battlefront. The army severely lacked medical provisions, equipment and drugs, but Seacole used herbal remedies and common sense to prevent infection.

In August 1856, Mary Seacole returned to live in London, but she was penniless and in poor health. Mary Seacole died on 14 May 1881, at 3 Cambridge Street (now Kendal Street), Paddington. For many years, her contribution to history was forgotten, but in 2004, Mary Seacole came first in an online poll of '100 Great Black Britons'. 'Mother' Seacole is acknowledged as the first nurse practitioner, a brave woman who battled racism and paved the way for diversity in nursing. A statue of Mary Seacole was erected in 2016, in the grounds of St Thomas' Hospital, London.

QUESTIONS

■ Easy

1. Cambridge Street becomes Kendal Street, Southwick Street becomes Titchborne Row, Southwick Crescent becomes Hyde Park Crescent. What does Watling Street become?

2. What shape does Sussex Square surround on the map?

■ Medium

3. Which building is like a snake?

4. Standing in a circle: SE has 3, NE has 4, SW has 0. How many does NW have?

■ Tricky

5. To the nearest 100m, how far apart are Marble Arch Underground station and the southern of the two Edgware Road Underground stations?

6. How many times does the word 'mews' appear on both maps in total?

■ Challenging

7. Start at the intersection of a street that would become a *Breaking Bad* actor if 'CRAN' were added with a road that's 148.5mm by 210mm. Turn right on a road when you encounter the first road that contains a part of the body that babies have more of than adults. Turn right again when you reach its 'newer' counterpart. Turn right yet again when you see Principal Skinner, and finally turn right one last time when you reach the second in line to the British throne. If you rotate your head so that the first line you drew is vertical, which letter have you traced out?

8. Which places on the map share the same consonants in the same order as the clues below? (For example, PADDINGTON shares the same consonants in the same order as PUDDING EATEN. The place labels are as they appear on the map, e.g. Gloucester Sq for Gloucester Square).

   AT HEEL, A KITE!

   BALLAST

   HEY, DO I PARK IT OR RACE?

   PROUDEST

   I SHALL BORE PAOLO

   ALIBI: NO AGOUTI

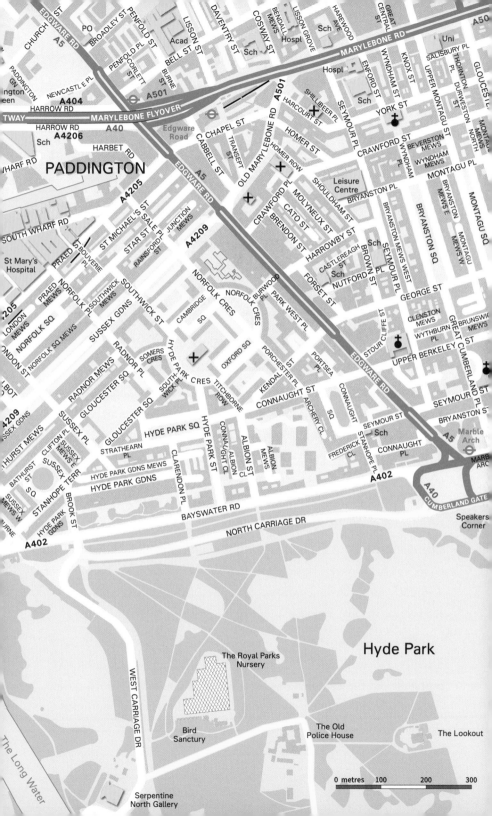

Map 33 VICTORIA DRUMMOND AND ERROL, PERTHSHIRE

A pioneering Scottish marine engineer, Victoria Alexandrina Drummond was born on 14 October 1894 in Megginch Castle. The Drummonds were very well connected, and Victoria was named after her godmother, Queen Victoria. At a young age, it was evident that Drummond had an aptitude for engineering and her father encouraged her to choose her own career. She was apprenticed at Northern Garage in Perth and had a supportive foreman and evening tuition in maths and engineering.

Drummond went on to work for the Caledon Shipbuilding & Engineering Company in Dundee, first as a pattern maker and then in the finishing shop. The newly formed Women's Engineering Society welcomed her in 1919, and she became the first female member of the Institute of Marine Engineers.

In 1927, she became the first woman in the world to obtain her Second Engineer's Certificate. Not content with her qualifications, Drummond repeatedly sat the examinations for the rank of Chief Engineer, but the examiners failed her at every attempt. One of her sponsors confronted the examining board who confessed that they had failed her because she was a woman. Despite this deliberate setback, Drummond persisted and finally passed her examinations for the rank of Chief Engineer in 1937. She became the first woman in that role on board a British merchant ship, the SS *Bonita* in 1939.

During World War II, Drummond served in the British Merchant Navy and commanded ships through dangerous waters, receiving the British Empire Medal for bravery and service. After the war, she continued to break boundaries in the maritime industry. She actively advocated for the advancement of women in engineering and belonged to several societies and professional organisations to improve standards of safety in the shipping industry.

Throughout her career, Drummond faced discrimination and scepticism from her male superiors, who doubted her abilities as a woman. However, her tenacity and strength proved to her colleagues that she was more than capable in the world of engineering.

In recognition of her achievements, Drummond became a Member of the Order of the British Empire in 1941 and was awarded the Lloyd's War Medal for Bravery at Sea. She also received an Honorary Doctorate of Science from the University of Glasgow in 1957.

Drummond retired in 1962 and spent time with her sisters Jean and Frances. She died on 25 December 1978 and was buried at Megginch Castle.

▓ Easy

1. Start with the number of the B-road south of Newburgh, add to it the number of the A-road north of Shipbriggs, and subtract the height of Ormiston Hill. What number is the result?

2. How many times are the four compass points (north, south, east and west) each mentioned, either on their own or as part of a larger word?

▓ Medium

3. On the map, what connects Hill, Mains, Park and Station?

4. Where would not be a good place to put all your money and savings, if you want to live?

▓ Tricky

5. What is the closest distance between the two railway lines in the north and south of the map?

6. Which Shakespearean character is a bit annoyed?

▓ Challenging

7. Start at a nonet of water sources. Travel in a straight line to a place named after a grassy area without any hills. Then go in a straight line to find a friend of the host of *Supermarket Sweep*. Then go in a straight line to have a fight with ABBA's Andersson. What letter have you traced out?

8. Which locations on the map have had their vowels removed and their consonants respaced?

DNF LN DRS

MR DG

BRN THY BNK

NC HC NNS

RM STN

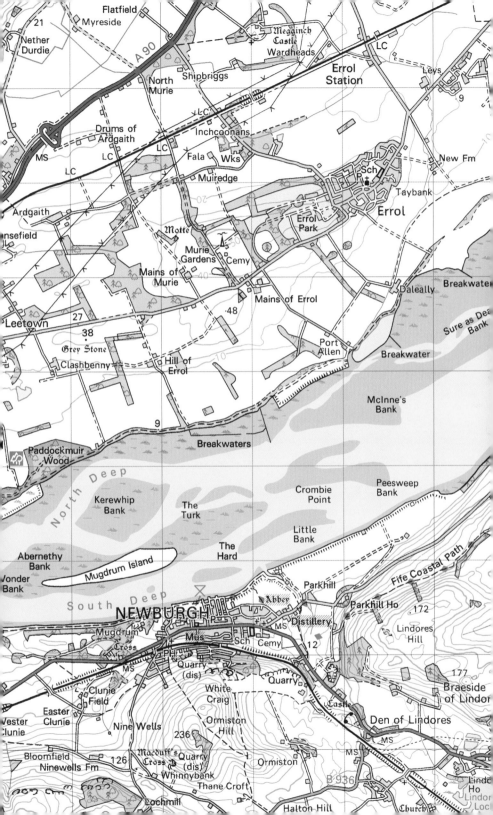

Map 34 ESMÉ KIRBY AND ERYRI (SNOWDONIA)

Born in Croydon on 31 August 1910, young Esmé Cummings was educated at Arne Hall School in Llandudno. Sir Frank Benson trained her in his Shakespeare Company, and Esmé followed her aspirations to become an actress. Drawn back to Wales because of her love of horses, she was busy running a riding school when she met her first husband, Thomas Firbank.

The couple married and Firbank wrote a book, *I Bought a Mountain* (1940), about their life in Dyffryn Mymbyr. Esmé was described as having delicate elfin features, but her strength and tenacity impressed and attracted Firbank. She tackled the Welsh Three Thousands Challenge and completed the circuit of fourteen peaks in nine hours and twenty-five minutes, only one hour behind her husband.

When World War II began, the marriage was dissolved and Firbank enlisted, leaving Esmé to run the farm alone. Major Peter Kirby visited the area and the two met and married, running the farm together until 1984, when they hired a manager.

Esmé fought several campaigns to stop commercial development near Eryri. She opposed the construction of a youth hostel and the development of a hydroelectric pipeline. Her public action saved the Cromlech Boulders on the roadside in Llanberis Pass, still used by climbers today.

Esmé founded the Snowdonia National Park Society in 1958, to prevent any further ideas of development in the area. By the late 1980s, she had fallen out with the board and stood down as chair. In retaliation, she formed the Esmé Kirby Snowdonia Trust in 1991 to complement the work of the society.

Peter supported Esmé and they worked hard to establish and maintain footpaths around the area, building footbridges on the Glyder Fach mountain path.

In her later years, Esmé campaigned for the control of grey squirrels and used highly controversial traps to stop their conquest of Anglesey. The greys had replaced the smaller native red squirrels. By 1998, only forty adult reds remained on the island. Esmé's intervention worked and twenty-five years later, there are over 700 red squirrels on the island.

On 18 October 1999, Esmé passed away in her farmhouse. She is buried on the mountainside at Dyffryn Mymbyr. In 2013 the National Trust acquired the 3,000-acre hill farm and added it to the 20,000 hectares already owned by the trust, safeguarding Eryri's future.

■ Easy

1. Which peak is 526m in altitude?

2. What separates an A-road and a B-road whose numbers differ by 4636?

■ Medium

3. How many symbols for nature reserves, represented by a duck, are on the map?

4. Which place on the map has a name made up of a hair product, an aquatic plant and a level of martial arts proficiency?

■ Tricky

5. What is the longest single-word place name on the map? (Discount any places with hyphens in their name.)

6. 726 to 690, 782 to 356. What's plane-ly in the middle?

■ Challenging

7. Which peak on the map has a name that, if you were to swap a mischievous fairy for the letters 'ISG', it would produce a controversial foodstuff?

8. Which locations on the map have had their vowels removed and their consonants respaced, and which one of these is a red herring and does not represent somewhere on the map?

   SN GRG

   CRN DDM LS BD

   RH YD

   GL SN FR YN PN TR

   NT TH SN

   PS SFB RGL SL YN

Map 35 JOHN LENNON AND LIVERPOOL

The city of Liverpool is synonymous with the band The Beatles, and all four members grew up in the city.

John Winston Lennon was born on 9 October 1940 to Julia and Alfred Lennon. They spent John's early life living at 9 Newcastle Road, but Alf was often away in the merchant navy and the marriage didn't last.

Julia struggled with parenthood, and eventually, her elder sister gained custody of John. He moved in with his Aunt Mimi and Uncle George in a semi-detached house, Mendips, 251 Menlove Avenue, Woolton. Julia visited regularly and taught her son to play the banjo and the ukulele. Tragically, she was hit by a car and killed in July 1958, when John was only seventeen.

Lennon did not do well in high school but accepted a place at the Liverpool College of Art in 1957. Academically, he struggled, but the experience probably broadened his outlook. Here, he met Cynthia Powell, who would become his first wife.

Lennon formed a skiffle band in 1956 called The Quarrymen. Paul McCartney joined a year later and introduced George Harrison, who was only fourteen at the time. They started to play rock and roll-inspired songs, and a few members quit the band, leaving John, Paul and George. In 1960, they changed their name to The Beatles.

The Beatles' music reflected the social and cultural changes of the era. Lennon started the 1960s writing pop tunes with catchy melodies, progressing into very experimental sounds by the end of the decade. In January 1969, The Beatles performed on the rooftop of their Apple Corps headquarters in London. The concert would be their last live performance together.

Lennon married the Japanese artist Yoko Ono in March 1969. They were prominent activists, staging a 'bed-in for peace' during their honeymoon at the Amsterdam Hilton, in protest against the Vietnam War. Their second bed-in event was staged a few months later in Montreal and ended in the spontaneous recording of 'Give Peace a Chance'. Lennon continued to be an activist for world peace until his untimely death.

On 8 December 1980, John and Yoko were returning to their apartment in the Dakota Building in New York when Lennon was fatally shot by Mark David Chapman.

Liverpool has numerous tributes to Lennon and his legacy. Most notably, in 2001 the airport was rebranded and named 'Liverpool John Lennon Airport'.

■ Easy

1. What is the only street on the map under which a tunnel runs along the entire length of it?

2. Which US state is the name of a street on the map?

■ Medium

3. Is the distance from the centre of the Roman Catholic cathedral to the triangulation point in the centre of the southern cathedral more or less than 1km?

4. Which label on the map, if you add an 'A' into it, was famously said by Kenneth Williams in *Carry On Cleo*?

■ Tricky

5. Which two streets, parallel and next to each other, are anagrams of each other aside from an extra 'P' in one of their names?

6. How many buildings with a bold outline lie, entirely or partly, between 100m and 125m in altitude?

■ Challenging

7. Start at the junction where an orange property and a green property in Monopoly intersect. Head west and turn left after going past someone who sounds like they could be Fitch's uncool partner. At a point where an elevation is given, turn right. Turn right again when you encounter a character played by Nicholas Lyndhurst. Keep going straight ahead, past two knolls, one nice and one tan and sad. Stop above a tunnel. If Pete is on your left, who could be on your right?

8. Which places on the map are represented by the alternate letter clues given below?

    _A_K_E_ S_U_R_

    _L_C_B_R_E _L_C_

    _I_D_R_ S_R_E_

    _O_P_R_S _I_L

    _A_R_L_U_H _A_E

Map 36 FREDDIE MERCURY AND WEMBLEY STADIUM

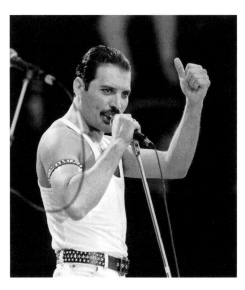

Freddie Mercury was a British musician and the lead vocalist of the rock band Queen. He was born Farrokh Bulsara on 5 September 1946, in Stone Town, Zanzibar (now part of Tanzania). The Bulsara family left Africa in 1964 during the Zanzibar Revolution and moved to Middlesex, England.

Mercury's musical talent was evident from an early age, but he studied graphic art and design at Ealing Art College. After meeting Brian May and Roger Taylor in 1970, they formed the band Queen, and bassist John Deacon joined a year later. Known for his extravagant costumes, theatrical style and stage presence, Mercury captivated audiences with a powerful vocal range that spanned four octaves.

Mercury was pursuing a solo career when Bob Geldof announced a concert to raise funds for famine relief in Ethiopia. Despite the tension, Queen pulled together and agreed to perform a twenty-minute set. Live Aid took place on 13 July 1985 at Wembley Stadium and was broadcast to 150 nations around the world. Queen played shortened versions of their six biggest hits, 'Bohemian Rhapsody', 'Radio Ga Ga', 'Hammer to Fall', 'Crazy Little Thing Called Love', 'We Will Rock You' and 'We Are the Champions'. They powerfully outperformed every other band on that day.

Societal attitudes towards LGBTQ+ individuals made it difficult for Freddie to be openly gay. However, he did eventually come out as bisexual and his unapologetic flamboyant persona broke barriers within the music industry and beyond. His personal life was often the subject of media attention, and he had high-profile relationships with both men and women.

Tragically, Mercury was diagnosed with HIV/AIDS in 1987 and his health rapidly declined. He died on 24 November 1991 at the age of forty-five. Freddie Mercury's musical legacy continues to inspire and he is widely regarded as one of the greatest rock singers of all time, receiving a posthumous induction into the Rock and Roll Hall of Fame in 2001.

Mercury also had a tremendous impact on popular culture and raised awareness of HIV/AIDS. After his death, the remaining members of Queen organised the Freddie Mercury Tribute Concert for AIDS Awareness, which took place at Wembley Stadium on 20 April 1992. Guests included Robert Plant, Roger Daltrey, Elton John and David Bowie, and the concert was broadcast worldwide to over a billion viewers. The band also founded The Mercury Phoenix Trust, which continues to raise money for research.

QUESTIONS

■ Easy

1. What purpose does this building have?

2. How many times does the word 'forty' appear on the map?

■ Medium

3. Which location on the map shares its first four letters with the first four letters of the largest city in the world, by population?

4. How much higher in altitude is the junction of Manor Drive and Wembley Hill Road than the junction of Oakington Avenue and the A4088?

■ Tricky

5. Which road on the map sounds like someone has prepared to propose?

6. What is the sum of all the numbers in the same grid square as Chalkhill Road? (Only include numbers written in digits; disregard any numbers written as words, such as 'Forty'.)

■ Challenging

7. What comes next in this sequence?

   – A fast food chain with the slogan 'Eat Fresh'

   – Get to one's feet

   – Rows of joined houses (twice)

   – ??

8. Rearrange these word fragments to form the names of six places on the grid:

   ACE / ASE / CAR / FIE / GES / HAR / HED / HOL / KCH / LDS / MAY / MID / NDU / OFI / PAL / PAR / RIA / ROA / ROW / STR / D / M / Y

RECOMMENDED THINGS TO DO

SCOTLAND

1. Take a visit to Scotland's capital, Edinburgh, and take a trip down the Royal Mile. Edinburgh's old town makes up part of the city's UNESCO World Heritage Site.

2. Set sail on Loch Katrine, upon the steamship *Sir Walter Scott* and take in the tranquil views of Loch Lomond and The Trossachs National Park.

WALES

1. Climb Wales' highest Mountain, Yr Wyddfa (Snowdon), which sits at a height of 1,085 metres and is located within Eryri (Snowdonia) National Park.

2. For something different, explore Devil's Bridge Falls near Aberystwyth. Three bridges have been built upon the previous bridge, with the most recent being built in 1901.

EAST ENGLAND

1. Explore Norfolk's Royal Coast. Visit the Royal Family's Sandringham Estate, which was bought by Queen Victoria over 150 years ago, and take a stroll along one of its sandy beaches located in the area.

2. Take to the water in The Broads National Park, where the water is gentle. Ideal to be explored by stand-up paddle board (SUP) or canoe.

LONDON

1. Regent's Park is an opportunity to absorb some green space and get away from the hustle and bustle of the city. Explore in the rose garden or take in the view from Primrose Hill.

2. Fancy a dip? Then take a swim in Hampstead Heath ponds. They are natural bathing ponds and one of London's best open-air swimming locations.

NORTH EAST

1. Want to drive across a tidal road and feel isolated, despite being so close to the mainland? Then Lindisfarne is the place to visit! The island is also known as Holy Island.

2. England's highest waterfall, High Force Waterfall, is in the North Pennines Area of Outstanding Natural Beauty, with a 21-metre drop into a plunge pool.

NORTH WEST

1. Visit the Lake District National Park, home to Scafell Pike (England's highest mountain) and Windermere (England's largest lake). Or you can snack on a Cumberland sausage or see Herdwick sheep.

2. If you are a fan of The Beatles' music then you must visit Liverpool, which is where it all started for them. Visit the Cavern Club where they performed and their popularity grew, or learn more by visiting The Beatles Story Museum.

SOUTH EAST

1. The White Cliffs of Dover are iconic and they are a symbol of Great Britain. Walking along the top of them is a must, and on a bright day you might be able to see France.

2. Want to spot a New Forest pony? These ponies are wild and can roam across the National Park, but they are owned. The park itself is a mixture of beautiful woodland and heathland.

SOUTH WEST

1. The Romans first invaded Britain in 55 BC, led by Julius Caesar. One of the best-preserved religious spas is the Roman Baths found in Bath. The natural thermal springs still run hot today.

2. Fancy taking to the water on a surfboard on the waves of the Atlantic Ocean? St Ives is a must for you. If you want a surf lesson, there's a number of local surf schools.

WEST MIDLANDS

1. Want to experience going back in time to the 1830s during the Industrial Revolution? You must visit the Black Country Living Museum – the largest open-air museum in England.

2. The Royal Air Force Museum at Cosford lets you explore and learn about aircraft from the start of the Royal Air Force right up to the present day. The museum is free and there is something for visitors of all ages.

YORKSHIRE & HUMBER

1. York is a medieval walled city, and the city itself was founded by the Romans. Exploring York on foot is the best way to see the city: visit York Minster, walk down the Shambles (best-preserved medieval shopping streets), or walk the city walls.

2. If you are in the area, then The Deep aquarium is a must visit. The Deep is Great Britain's largest aquarium and is located in Hull. Learn about sea and marine life from over 4,000 species of fish, sharks, penguins and more.

Loch Katrine

Edinburgh

Lindisfarne

Lake District
National Park

High Force
Waterfall

York

The Deep Aquarium

Liverpool

Yr Wyddfa
(Snowdon)

Sandringham
Estate

The Royal Air Force Museum

Black Country
Living Museum

The Broad
National Park

Devil's Bridge
Falls

Hampstead Heath
Ponds

Bath

Regents Park

The White Cliffs
of Dover

The New Forest

St Ives

SOLUTIONS

MAP
1

1. 3

2. Cane Lane

3. Charlton – as Bobby and Jack Charlton were members of England's winning team

4. The oddly shaped building. Denchworth Road Bridge is between 75m and 80m in altitude, the building is between 80m and 85m in altitude. The building can be found west of Elms Farm and east of a label saying A417

5. 11. The S of 'Spr', ORY of 'Factory', CH and O of Grove Technology Park, M of the Museum, OV of Grove Bridge Farm and C of Crab Hill Lane

6. 8 (Rifle Range, Cane Lane, Elms Farm, Crab Hill, The Ham, The Ark, Lark Hill (twice))

7. 2

8. Crab Hill (BAR reversed in CHILL), Charlton (CHART around L, and ON), Ickleton Road (anagram of NICK TORE LOAD), Rifle Range (RIFLE – to look through, and RANGE – array)

MAP
2

1. Newfield House

2. Quarrelton (ton = 100)

3. Northwards (as evidenced by the decreasing altitude in the contour lines)

4. A cup and ring (Dwayne Johnson is known as The Rock and there is a label on the map 'Cup & Ring marked Rock')

5. 80m. The northern Windyhill is at 20m altitude, the southern Windyhill is at 100m altitude

6. Low Bardrain (LOW, as in sad, BARD, Shakespeare, RAIN sounds like REIGN, rules)

7. Phoenix Business Park (Mon (short day) just above ELDERS LIE (seniors don't tell the truth), White House farm (where Bush bushes could grow). There are 6 Craigs, so three roundabouts)

8. The third one is the red herring with no place on the map that corresponds to it. The other four are: Linwood, Glenpatrick, Newfield House, Leitchland Farm

MAP
3

1. Parc Sycharth

2. Mynydd y Bryn (at the 320m contour in the NE of the map)

3. Belan, 200m contour

4. 400m (The footbridges east of Coed Ty-gwyn are ~380m apart, the one in the middle being
    equidistant from the other two)

5. Sycamore Cottage (sounds like SICKER MORE)

6. 24: Pont Ty-newydd, Pyllau r-meirch, Priddbwll-mawr, Tynewedd, Groesffordd, Mynydd y
    Bryn, Bwrdd Tre'r-Arglwydd, Blanhigfa Ddu, Motte & Bailey, Allt Goch, Pen-yr-allt,
    Yr Allt, Abercynllaith, Quarry, Cae-Adda Wood, Glan-yr-afon Cottage, Coed Abercynllaith,
    Penisarmynydd, Llanerchemrys, Sycamore Cottage, Mill Farm, Pen-y-bont Llanerch Emrys,
    Pen-y-bont Hall, Gelli Lwyd

7. Golfa, and it sounds like 'golfer' (e.g. Tiger Woods)

8. Coed Maestanyglwyden, Nant Goch, Blanhigfa Ddu, Bwrdd Tre'r-Arglwydd

MAP
4

1. 6

2. Frying pans

3. There are two more plantations on the map than commons (8 plantations: Kettle, Castle, Uphams, Crook, Island, Wheathill, Squabmoor, Dalditch; 6 commons: Colaton Raleigh, Woodbury, Bicton, East Budleigh, Withycombe Raleigh, Shortwood)

4. Rushmoor Wood (sounding like Mount Rushmore in the USA)

5. 105m

6. Exmouth Archery Club

7. Picnic site

8. Big Wood, Bystock Fishponds, Four Firs, Hayes Lane, Yettington

MAP
5

1. Beacon Hill Road

2. Leith House (after Prue Leith – and she could visit Leith House Crossing Cottage for a bit of variety for a vacation in the summer)

3. 31 (7+24)

4. 8

5. School

6. These are all places with REMAINS (i.e. against Brexit) on the map. A CROSS, Charlotte CHURCH and St Mary's Friary

7. 9 (Nelson's birthplace -> EastEnders without ERS, turn left, River Burn, Dismantled Railway, Reservoir)

8. Crabbe Hall Farm, Gravelpit Hill, Bellamy's Lane, Sewage Works

MAP
6

1. S (Queen Street and Bishop Street)

2. Military Row

3. Mill Dam Barracks

4. Little Britain Street

5. Cinder Track (Cinderella without Ella)

6. 1,550m

7. 11

8. F, V, X

MAP

7

1. 50m and 60m

2. 7

3. Falleninch

4. 3,000m

5. 5 – head on the A9 to the M9 J11, get off at J10 and take the A811 to King's Knot

6. St Ninians (which becomes St Trinian's, a school created by Ronald Searle)

7. The memorial to Gromit's owner (Wallace Monument) is the odd one out. The others – Fort (strength, in French), Castle and Standing Stone – are all written in Gothic font on the map, while Wallace Monument isn't

8. The red herring is STR LN GM SS, which represents STIRLING MOSS, the racing driver. The others represent the map locations of Bearside, Logie Villa, Park of Keir, Skeoch and Airthrey Castle

MAP
8

1. Footbridge

2. Queen's Dock

3. On Salthouse Lane is Sailors' Home, and a 'salt' is a nickname for a sailor

4. Land of Green Ginger (Ginger Spice, green meaning envious)

5. On the old map, Church Lane (Charlotte Church) becomes Liberty Lane (freedom)

6. These are the names of various mills on the old map: Oil (has the nickname black gold), Saw (horror-film franchise), Phoenix (mythological bird) and Alexandria (from the Library at Alexandria being one of the Seven Wonders of the Ancient World)

7. 3 times. You cross water 7 times and you have drawn the number 4

8. Spyvee Street, Charterhouse Lane, Garrison Side, Princes Dock Street, Lockwood Street, King Edward Street

MAP
9

1. 6

2. Timber

3. 9

4. Speen Road (becoming SPLEEN)

5. 130 (10 farms: Great Moseley, Little Moseley, Orchard, Boss Lane, Coombe's, Hogtrough, Naphill, Church, Downley, Manor; 13 woods: Little Stocking, Chalkpit, Gomms, Provost, Oaks, Flagmore, Woodcock, Hanging, Common, Millfield, Little Tinker's, Great Tinker's, Green)

6. Adam – the others all appear in place names on the map

7. S (Start at 179m, 180 = perfect three-dart score; Hunt's Hill for Helen Hunt; Stocking Lane)

8. Coombe's Orchards, Middle Lodge, Longrove Plantations, Sports Ground, Downley Common

MAP
10

1. They're all circular

2. Park Street

3. Temple of Health / Temple of Diana (The Temple of Diana was mislabelled on the old map)

4. These are all words that go before dwellings to make the names of four locations: Combe Lodge, Burleigh House and Thatch Cottage

5. Fair Rosamund's Well

6. 2,750m

7. N (Seven Arches, Grand Bridge, Fourteen Acre Clump)

8. (Old map) Infirmary, Mission Hall, Park Street; (New map) Column of Victory, Dog Kennel Hill, Icehouse Clump

MAP
11

1. Keble College

2. Logic Lane

3. 42 (There are 6 places of worship with a tower, 6 with a spire, minaret or dome, and 6 without a tower, spire, minaret or dome)

4. 4165, 4144 and 420. These are the numbers of the A-roads that travel the old route of the A423.

5. Beef Lane, which is in Pembroke (college) on the map

6. Gloucester. Gloucester Street connects Beaumont Street (*beau mont* meaning beautiful mountain in French) and Red Lion Square (Red Lion being a common pub name and square = multiplied by itself, like a square number)

7. A (blue) boar. Draw one line from Baltic Wharf (very cold) to the place on the new map that corresponds to the convent on South Parks Road on the old map. Draw another line from Corden Crescent (James Corden, *The Late Late Show* host in the US until 2023) to the Western Library (occidental means western). The lines cross at Blue Boar Street

8. Ruskin College, Albert Street, Pitt Rivers, Gas Street, New College School, Oriel College

MAP
12

1. Quad biking

2. 2m

3. 5

4. 7,500m

5. 67

6. Pensyflog (GOLF is written backwards in it)

7. Boston Lodge (there are two cemeteries, and there are four churches in a row marked on the map that you cross)

8. WEASEL VOWEL is the odd one out, which is an anagram of WE LOVE WALES. The others are anagrams of: Erwsuran, Borth-y-Gest, Portmeirion and Gorllwynuchaf

MAP

13

1. Rheilffordd (It must be in the label 'Bala Lake Railway / Rheilffordd Llyn Tegid', but not in the label above it 'Bala Lake / Llyn Tegid', hence it is Rheilffordd)

2. 164. These are altitudes given along the A494, moving from SW to NE

3. Lovers' Walk

4. Pentre-duldog

5. 18 (10, 20 and 30m depths in the lake. 180, 200, 240, 250, 280, 290, 300, 310, 320, 340, 350, 400, 430, 450, 500m contours)

6. 9km

7. 2 (Natural Resources Wales in the SE of the map. Ford is the 38th president. The hill has a height of 360m and likely has 360 degrees of views, at least when it isn't cloudy)

8. Pantymarch, Pont Mwnwgl-y-llyn, Nant Hafhesp, Gwastadros, Tomen Y Bala, Cornelau

MAP
14

1. 9

2. Bowburn

3. 6,924 (100+61+177+163+132+6291)

4. Mainsforth, at 10 letters

5. Green (Cookson's Green on the map, in relation to author Catherine Cookson)

6. 193m (at the trig point in the NE of the map)

7. Motel

8. Garmondsway (anagram of DRAGON SAW MY), Sprucely (sounds like SPRUCE LEE, lee meaning shelter), Cassop (hidden in orCAS, SO Pretty), Metal Bridge (Iron is METAL, initially gladly = G in BRIDE for BRIDGE), A1(M) which looks like AIM (point)

MAP
15

1. Factory

2. North (7 to the north: Coopers' Farm, Quobwell Farm, Griffins Barn Farm, Home Farm, White Lodge Farm, Filands Farm, Marsh Farm. 5 to the south: Thornhill Farm, Danielswell Farm, Arches Farm, Home Farm, Lawn Farm)

3. Wind pump

4. A429, which connects two Home Farms, one in the north and one in the south of the map

5. They are all bridges (Cow Bridge, Holloway Bridge, Back Bridge)

6. Dismantled Railway – dismantled is an anagram indicator cryptically, and WARY ALI is an anagram of Railway

7. 6. Travel from Lea House (as in Lea and Perrins) to Solar Panels to Filands (the plural of FINLAND if the first N is removed), and you will cross water six times

8. Airfield, Avon Mills, Coopers' Farm, Engineering Campus, Tetbury Hill Gardens. HER RED RING is the odd one out (it is an anagram of RED HERRING)

MAP
16

1. 8

2. 5,040 (4256+425+359)

3. Cwm Tyswg (nearby is Cwm Tysswg)

4. 6

5. Pound, in Waun y Pound (travel from Georgetown, the capital of Guyana, to Rassau, which is one letter away from Nassau, the capital of the Bahamas)

6. Dukestown (as in the Grand old DUKE of York)

7. Patch. Start at Burial Ground written in Gothic script and head towards Mount Pleasant. Move to Cefn Manmoel, go up ten diamonds, then go west 2km

8. Cruglwyn, Festival Park, Glyncoed, Troedrhiwfuwch

MAP
17

1. Brighton Street, Bristo Street and Bristo Place (making Bristol)

2. 290.5ft (at George Heriot's Hospital School)

3. Volunteer Drill Hall

4. 1628 (as part of George Heriot's Hospital School)

5. J, X and Z

6. 9

7. 137 (58 properties face on to George Square, 16 on the southern side and 14 on the other three sides, and there are 79 tree symbols in George Square)

8. Museum (Start at the intersection of Chrichton and Charles Street. Go up to intersection of Candlemaker Row and Merchant Street. Move south to Chambers Street and go to the museum)

MAP
18

1. 28m (from 91m to 119m)

2. Keepers Cottage (as in 'Finders keepers, losers weepers')

3. 110m, which appears 8 times (120m is next, with 5 times)

4. Ermine Street (ermine being the white winter coat of a stoat)

5. 1.35km

6. Sheep dip, mint sauce being a dip that lamb is traditionally eaten with

7. Wellspring Plantation (Rhyming high factory = MILL HILL. Otters live in a holt, cockles are molluscs. Kris Kardashian's maiden name is Houghton. In the middle of the two, 'x marks the spot' like, is Wellspring Plantation)

8. The Grotto, Parson's Holt, Cringle Plantations, Easton Cold Store

MAP

19

1. 120m (in the northwest of the new map)

2. Derbyshire (referring to the Derbyshire Extensions in two places on the map)

3. Burton Joyce (referencing the first names of Richard Burton and James Joyce)

4. NOINU – these are part of the label 'Parly. Co. Div. Union & R.D. By.', written in reverse

5. There are 5 places of worship on the old map, of which 4 are also on the new map. One chapel is not marked on the new map

6. 12

7. 8

8. PITCH FERNS HERE is the red herring, which is an anagram of THE FRESH PRINCE (Carlton is a character in the sitcom *The Fresh Prince of Bel-Air*). The others are, in order: Adbolton, Trent Field Plantation, Locomotive Shed, Cotgrave Place, Polser Brook

MAP
20

1. 11 (Thames Path runs through 7 grid squares and there are 4 stations on the map)

2. Seething Wells

3. 2,199 (310+358+308+309+364+307+243)

4. J

5. Old Icehouse (an igloo being an 'ice house')

6. 81

7. You would not encounter regal cat sounds (Royal Mews). You would encounter something dedicated to a confused naiad (Diana Fountain, confused naiad = anagram naiad to become Diana), sweeping tufts (Broom Clumps) and the Shoemaker's Way (Cobbler's Path)

8. Bushy House, Hampton Wick, Heron Pond, Oval Plantation, Parkfield

MAP
21

1. Two cloth and silk mills and a gas works

2. Cain's Folly (Cain killed Abel in the Bible)

3. Blackpool (referencing Blackpool Corner)

4. 4

5. River Lim (Jordan and Jericho lie both sides of a river in the old map, and the new map has the label R Lim)

6. Something belonging to actor Liu (for example). These are clues to CANARY, BROAD and LONG, which are the names of ledges on the coast moving southwest, making sure to inspect both maps. The next one is LUCY'S Ledge

7. A dragon (Woodcote, Monarch's Way, the A35 where it is 143m in altitude, roundabout, Fern Hill, Dragon's Hill)

8. Stammery Hill (Mound said with a stammer), Catherston Leweston (anagram of NEWCASTLE SET ON THOR), Cumberland Cottage, Fishpond Bottom, Sleech Wood (WOOD after/by S (small) LEECH (bloodsucker))

MAP
22

1. There is now a footbridge there

2. Shoplatch

3. 166ft, equivalent to approximately 50.6m

4. Mount Street

5. a – Berwick; b – Porthill; c – Claremont

6. Where an outdoor show is held (for example). These are clues to West, Mid, Agricultural – so the next clue is for the word SHOWGROUND

7. 8 (Grecian Portal, Tudor Gate, Nettles Lane, Drinkwater Street, Greenhill Avenue, Welsh Bridge, The Dingle)

8. Tannery, Town Walls, Mount Cottage, Sand Pit, Copthorne Crest

MAP
23

1. 200m

2. Roundabouts on the A24

3. 11 (There are 9 parking symbols, but 2 of them point to 2 car parks)

4. Tower Hill

5. These are all hills. The clues are to Bury, Box, Root and Rose; and Bury Hill, Box Hill, Root Hill and Rose Hill are all located on the map

6. 83. These are the heights in metres of the six triangulation points on the map, in descending order

7. North Holmwood (Start at Juniper Top, travel southwest one grid square, then east two grid squares, south five grid squares as 'Fm' does appear, then follow the road as directed)

8. Druids Cove, Milton Court, Tanner's Brook, Abinger Forest, Brockham Warren

MAP
24

1. Ailstone (becoming HAILSTONE)

2. Clopton Bridge (you are looking south, so your left is east on the map)

3. Spire/minaret/dome, based on the marking in its location on the new map

4. Wind pumps

5. Small place of worship. These are clues to streets radiating off a junction on the old map with ELY Street to the west, HIGH Street to the north, SHEEP Street to the east, and CHAPEL Street to the south

6. 85m. The book by Stella Gibbons is *Cold Comfort Farm*

7. 4632439. These are pairs of numbers of roads that go off the edge of the map, starting in the top left and moving clockwise. A3400 and A46 -> 340046. A439 and B4086 -> 4394086. A422 and A3400 -> 4223400. The next two are B4632 and B439 -> 4632439

8. Bull Street, Tiddington, Hollow Meadow, Gospel Oak, Warwick Road Nursery, One Elm Bridge, Lucy's Locks

MAP
25

1. Gala Hill

2. A7

3. Roman Park

4. Langlee (which becomes Ang Lee)

5. H_2O that isn't alive (or any similar description) – these are descriptions of the names of pools on the River Tweed, moving downstream to the northeast: Harp Pool, Hindshouse Pool, Mosshouse Pool, Deadwater Pool

6. 2,000m

7. G (Glenn Close, so Glenfield; The Shepherd's Cottage)

8. Gun Knowe Loch, Newfaan, Abbotsmoss, Englishmen's Sike, Upper Faldonside

MAP
26

1. 13

2. Holborn (A40 meets the A4200, 40 x 105 = 4,200)

3. William IV

4. 750m (the closest points between Denmark Street and Portugal Street)

5. Langley Street, as the CIA have their headquarters in Langley, Virginia, USA

6. A. It will turn WILD CT into WILD CAT, which describes a tiger (Floral Street, Bow Street, Wellington Street, Russell Street, Drury Lane, Parker Street, Kingsway (King sway), Wild Ct)

7. 9 (Gloucester, Oxford, Lincoln, Newport, Leicester, Southampton, Exeter, Durham, York. Other places are mentioned on the map but they are not cities. Litchfield Street is on the map, but the city is spelled Lichfield)

8. The Mall, Kings College, British Museum, Victoria Embankment, Red Lion Square, Festival Pier

MAP
27

1. Half Acre

2. 3 (High Birks Beck, Pinch Beck, Pitty Beck)

3. (B) 6144 (the almanac is Wisden, add an L to make Wilsden Road in the northeast of the map)

4. Pudding Hill

5. A (Long Lane, Dean Lane, Egypt)

6. These are all middle words in three-word farm names: Well Heads Farm, Squirrel Hill Farm or Whinney Hill Farm, New Holland Farm, Nettle Hole Farm, Allan House Farm or Carr House Farm or Shay House Farm

7. 2,600m

8. Harrop Edge, Upper Pikeley, Headley Golf Club, Salt Pie

MAP
28

1. False – most begin with M (Mus, Mus's, Maiden Castle, Max Gate) but one begins with W (Wolfeton Ho)

2. Durnovaria – it is written below the word DORCHESTER on the map. (The letter 'v' was also used for the letter 'u' in Roman times)

3. 80m (60m near Winterborne Came and 140m near Wolfeton Clump)

4. Charlton Down

5. Conquer Barrow

6. These are all farms with the word Higher in the title – Higher Burton Fm (Richard Burton narrated Jeff Wayne's musical version of *The War of the Worlds*), Higher Came Fm (CAMEL without its last letter) and Higher Kingston Fm (Kingston is the capital of Jamaica)

7. 9

8. Wolf is the red herring. The locations on the map are Cow Den, Hardy Way, Haydon Hill, Leap Gate, Pound Bury and Winterborne Herringston

MAP
29

1. They are all woods

2. 314 (100+50+47+66+51)

3. Belle Isle (Belle from *Beauty and the Beast*)

4. Tower

5. On the Lilies of the Valley islands – *Convallaria majalis* is the scientific name for the flower lily of the valley

6. Cuckoo (Cuckoo Brow Wood), Crow (Crow Holme), Hawk (Hawkshead Flat and Hawkrigg Farm), Sparrow (Sparrow How Wood)

7. M (Eel House, Oatmeal Crag, Argent Close, (270) trig point, Bellman Landing)

8. Stone is the fragment left over. The constructed place names are Colthouse Heights, Cuckoo Brow Wood, Crabtree Cottages and Long Parrock

MAP
30

1. City of Glasgow College

2. (St) Mungo

3. 3: There is a Paul Street (Paul McCartney), a John Knox Street (John Lennon), George Street (George Harrison), but no Ringo (though RING is mentioned in Springburn Road)

4. Bridge of Sighs

5. Bell Street (as bells toll)

6. 384. The buildings look like 3 and 2, making the number 32. There are 11 P.H. and P.Hs. markings on the old map. 32 x 12 = 384

7. B (Black Street by Bowling Green, black and green are worth 7 and 3 in snooker respectively; Walls Street; Saint Nicholas's Hospital; junction of Mason and Weaver Street; M8 southernmost blue line)

8. On the new map: Rottenrow, Necropolis Cemetery, Sighthill Circus. On the old map: Lock Hospital, Barony Street. On both maps but in different locations: Bowling Green

MAP
31

1. The Royal Navy (Britannia Royal Navy College)

2. The Laundry

3. 180m and 400ft. 180m is higher (400ft is just over 120m)

4. Boohay

5. 179m. These obtuse indications of the height markers on the A379 (99m) and B3205 (104m) are either side of the hill to the north of Croftland. The answer is the height of this hill, 179m

6. 17: Yalberton, Goodrington, Waddeton Court, Waddeton, Galmpton Warborough, Galmpton, Galmpton Creek, Churston Sta(tion), Alston Fm, Anchor Stone, Lupton Park, Bruckton, Downton, Chipton, Lower Norton, Norton, Cotton

7. E

8. Greenway House (WAY in GREENHOUSE), Galmpton Creek (anagram of CREAM KEPT LONG), Kingswear (KING'S WEAR), Parson's Mud (Anagram of DUMPS around ARSON), Saltern Cove (SALT, ERNE around CO and V), Dittisham (DITTY with last letter removed, IS, HAM)

MAP
32

1. Edgware Road – these are the new names for various roads on the new map compared to the old map

2. Circle

3. Serpentine North Gallery

4. 6 – these are the number of trees in the green areas (not on paths) in the quadrants around the circle in the burial ground on the old map

5. 900m

6. 29 (20 on the new map, 9 on the old map)

7. P. Bryanston St (becomes Bryan Cranston from *Breaking Bad* – there are a few Bryanstons but only one is a street that connects with the A5) and A5 (paper size), Old Marylebone Road (babies have around 300 bones, adults have 206), Marylebone Road, Seymour Place (Seymour Skinner from *The Simpsons*), George Street (Prince George)

8. The Lookout, Bell St, Hyde Park Terrace, Praed St, Shillibeer Pl, Albion Gate

MAP
33

1. 790 (The roads are the B936 and A90, and Ormiston Hill is 236m in altitude. 936 + 90 – 236 = 790)

2. 2 North, 1 South, 1 East, 1 West

3. Errol (These are words that form parts of places on the map if you include the word Errol – Hill of Errol, Mains of Errol, Errol Station and Errol Park)

4. Sure as Death Bank

5. 5km, between the leftmost level crossing on the northern railway line, and by the public house and church in Newburgh in the south

6. Macduff (Macduff's Cross)

7. P (Nine Wells, Flatfield, Daleally, Clashbenny)

8. Den of Lindores, Muiredge, Abernethy Bank, Inchcoonans, Ormiston

MAP
34

1. Pen y Bedw

2. Afon (River) Conwy separates the A470 and the B5106

3. 7

4. Gellilydan (GEL + LILY + DAN)

5. Penrhyndeudraeth (16 letters)

6. 747. If you draw a line between the peaks with heights of 726m and 690m, and another between the ones at 782m and 356m, they cross at a peak with a height of 747m, and 747 is a common nickname for a plane

7. FOEL-FRAS, which would become FOIS GRAS if ELF was replaced with ISG

8. Eisingrug, Carnedd Moel-siabod, Rhyd, Glasinfryn Pentir, (red herring), Pass of Aberglaslyn. The fifth one is a red herring as NT TH SN represents NOT THIS ONE

MAP
35

1. Great George Street

2. Maryland

3. Less (about 880m)

4. INFMY (As in 'Infamy, infamy, they've all got it in for me')

5. PROSPECT Street and PRESCOT Street

6. 10

7. Anne, Charlotte or Emily; as they are famous Brontë sisters (Junction of Vine and Oxford Streets, Abercromby Square, 162 elevation marker, Rodney Street past Mount Pleasant and Brownlow Hill, stopping at the junction of Russell Street, Tong Street (Pete Tong is a famous DJ) and Bronte Street)

8. Falkner Square, Blackburne Place, Gildart Street, Copperas Hill, Fairclough Lane

MAP
36

1. TV Studios

2. 4 (Forty Bridge, Forty Close, Forty Avenue, Forty Lane)

3. Tokyngton Community Cen(tre) – Tokyo is the largest city in the world by population

4. 46m (Manor Drive / Wembley Hill Road is at 179m, Oakington Avenue / A4088 is at 133m)

5. Neeld Cres(cent) (sounds like 'Kneeled')

6. 13,740 (127+152+4089+200+175+133+4089+110+4565+100)

7. Empire Stadium. These are clues to Subway, Stand, Terraces (written twice), labels written around the Empire Stadium getting closer to the pitch, so the answer is the central label itself (or a clue leading towards it, such as 'Ottoman Arena')

8. Carriage Shed, Harrow Road, Mayfields, Midholm, Palace of Industry, Park Chase

YOUR
NOTES

ORDNANCE SURVEY MAP INFORMATION

The Ordnance Survey Puzzle Book: Legends and Landmarks features our celebrated OS Explorer mapping, enlarged slightly from the familiar scale of 1:25 000 to 1:20 000 to improve the puzzle experience. The iconic OS Explorer map is used daily by thousands of people, from ramblers to rock climbers. The first time maps were produced at the 1:25 000 scale (2.5 inches on the map being equivalent to 1 mile on the ground, or 4cm to 1km) was in the early twentieth century, but back then only the military had access to this level of detail on a paper map; the first military map from Ordnance Survey covered East Anglia.

Mapping was extremely important during the two world wars, but it wasn't until 1938 that it was suggested that a series of maps be produced for the general public. The thinking was that if this idea took off in schools, then the mapping might eventually cover the whole of Great Britain to give outdoors enthusiasts unrivalled access to the countryside. The first experimental (or provisional) maps at this scale appeared after World War II ended in 1945.

Interest in leisure time spent in the countryside began to grow, and more consideration was given to 1:25 000 mapping. In 1972, the first Outdoor Leisure (OL) map was published, of the Dark Peak area of the Peak District, and subsequently other OL maps were published, concentrating on the National Parks and Areas of Outstanding Natural Beauty. As a result of the success of the Outdoor Leisure maps, many other maps were redesigned. These were called Pathfinders, and they covered England and Wales, showing all public rights of way, and making it easier to plan walking routes.

The first OS Explorer maps were published in 1994, replacing the popular Pathfinder series and making our maps even more user-friendly. On average the OS Explorer maps covered three times the area of the Pathfinders and were six times bigger than the original Outdoor Leisure maps at this scale. The additional tourist and leisure information – including viewpoints, pubs and picnic sites – resulted in an amazing level of detail.

By 2003, every Pathfinder and Outdoor Leisure map had been converted to the OS Explorer series and in 2004, following the Countryside and Rights of Way Act 2000, areas of open access were depicted. These days, if you buy an OS Explorer map you also get a free mobile download to use in our award-winning OS Maps app.

Not sure which leisure map you need for your next adventure? Here's a handy comparison:

OS Explorer 1:25 000 (4cm to 1km or 2.5 inches to the mile) is the nation's most popular leisure map. It features footpaths, rights of way and open-access land, and is recommended for walking, running and horse riding. The OS Explorer map covers a smaller area than the OS Landranger map, but presents the landscape in more detail, aiding navigation and making it the perfect accompaniment on an adventure. It also highlights tourist information and points of interest, including viewpoints and pubs.

OS Landranger 1:50 000 (2cm to 1km or 1.25 inches to the mile) aids the planning of the perfect short break in Great Britain and is a vital resource for identifying opportunities in both towns and countryside. It displays larger areas of the country than OS Explorer, making it more suitable for touring an area by car or by bicycle, helping you access the best an area has to offer.

OS Road 1:250 000 (1cm to 2.5km or 1 inch to 4 miles) is ideal for navigating and planning any road journey, and helps you get to your destination. The range covers the whole of Great Britain and shows all motorways, primary routes and A-roads, plus detailed tourist information including National Parks, World Heritage Sites and a useful town and city gazetteer.

ORDNANCE SURVEY SHEET INDEX

	Puzzle map legend	Location	OS map sheet			Centre point	1 km reference
1	Alfred the Great	Wantage, Oxfordshire	170	174	8	SU 39800 87900	SU 39 87
2	William Wallace	Elderslie, Renfrewshire	342	64	3	NS 44230 63070	NS 44 63
3	Owain Glyndwr	Sycharth, Llansilin, Powys	240	126	6	SJ 20530 25880	SJ 20 25
4	Walter Raleigh	Hayes Barton, Devon	115	192	7	SY 5100 85200	SY 5 85
5	Horatio Nelson	Burnham Thorpe, Norfolk	251	132	5	TF 85610 40635	TF 85 40
6	Isambard Kingdom Brunel	Portsmouth, Hampshire	OL 3	196	8	SZ 63300 99550	SZ 63 99
7	David Stirling	Bridge of Allan, Stirling	366	57	3	NS 78950 97570	NS 78 97
8	William Wilberforce	Kingston upon Hull, Yorkshire	293	107	4	TA 10170 28690	TA 10 28
9	Benjamin Disraeli	Hughenden, High Wycombe	172	165	8	SU 86430 95530	SU 86 95
10	Winston Churchill	Blenheim Palace, Oxfordshire	180	164	5	SP 44120 16070	SP 44 16
11	Robert Smallbones	Trinity College, Oxford	180	164	5	SP 51500 06500	SP 51 06
12	T E Lawrence	Tremadog, Gwynedd, Wales	OL 18	124	6	SH 56170 40175	SH 56 40
13	Betsi Cadwaladr	Llyancil, Wales	OL 23	125	6	SH 91450 34950	SH 91 34
14	Elizabeth Barrett Browning	Coxhoe, County Durham	305	93	4	NZ 32160 35650	NZ 32 35
15	Alice Seeley Harris	Malmesbury, Wiltshire	168	173	6	ST 93070 87400	ST 93 87
16	Nye Bevan	Tredegar, Monmouthshire	166	161	6	SO 14070 08970	SO 14 08
17	The Edinburgh Seven	Edinburgh	350	66	3	NT 25800 73300	NT 25 73
18	Isaac Newton	Woolsthorpe-by-Colsterworth	247	130	5	SK 92430 24380	SK 92 24
19	Mary Wortley Montagu	Holme Pierrepoint Hall, Notts	260	129	5	SK 62650 39250	SK 62 39
20	Michael Faraday	Hampton Court Palace	161	176	8	TQ 15720 68500	TQ 15 68
21	Mary Anning	Lyme Regis, Dorset	116	193	7	SY 34250 92100	SY 34 92
22	Charles Darwin	Shrewsbury, Shropshire	241	126	6	SJ 48550 13070	SJ 48 13
23	Marie Stopes	Dorking, Surrey	146	187	8	TQ 16500 49370	TQ 16 49
24	William Shakespeare	Stratford-upon-Avon, Warks	205	150	5	SP 20340 54755	SP 20 54
25	Sir Walter Scott	Abbotsford, near Galashiels	338	73	3	NT 50790 34300	NT 50 34
26	JMW Turner	Covent Garden, London	173	176	8	TQ 30370 80900	TQ 30 80
27	Emily Bronte	Thornton, West Yorksire	288	104	4	SE 10030 32750	SE 10 32
28	Thomas Hardy	Dorchester, Dorset	OL 15	194	7	SY 70450 89900	SY 70 89
29	Beatrix Potter	Near Sawrey, Cumbria	OL7	97	4	SD 37025 95555	SD 37 95
30	Charles Rennie Mackintosh	Townhead, Glasgow	342	64	3	NS 60170 65690	NS 60 65
31	Agatha Christie	Galmpton, Devon	OL 20	202	7	SX 87200 54760	SX 87 54
32	Mary Seacole	Paddington, London	173	176	8	TQ 27395 81180	TQ 27 81
33	Victoria Drummond	Errol, Perthshire	380	59	3	NO 25300 22900	NO 25 22
34	Esmé Kirby	Snowdonia National Park	OL 17	115	6	SH 69500 57100	SH 69 57
35	John Lennon	Liverpool	275	108	4	SJ 35700 90330	SJ 35 90
36	Freddie Mercury	Wembley Stadium, London	173	176	8	TQ 19365 85530	TQ 19 85

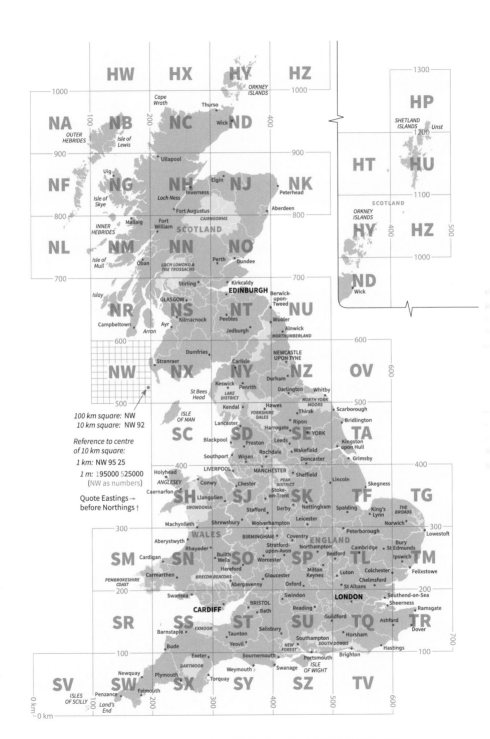

CREDITS

Seven Dials would like to thank everyone at Orion who worked on the publication of *The Ordnance Survey Puzzle Book: Legends And Landmarks* in the UK.

Editorial: Georgia Goodall, George Brooker, Jane Hughes.

Copy editor: Ian Greensill. Proofreader: Katie Crous.

Production: Sarah Cook.

Design: Helen Ewing, Julyan Bayes, Natalie Dawkins.

Finance: Nick Gibson, Jasdip Nandra.

Contracts: Dan Herron.

Sales: Jen Wilson, Esther Waters, Victoria Laws.

Operations: Jo Jacobs.

PICTURE CREDITS

Alamy p20, 24, 25, 28, 32, 33, 36, 37, 40, 41, 44, 45, 54, 66, 76, 77, 85, 89, 93, 106, 118, 119, 136, 137, 140, 141, 144, 145, 148, 178, 179

Esme Kirby p170

Creative Commons 40 Llywelyn2000 p29

Creative Commons, University of Edinburgh, Work Record ID:0009176 p92

Getty p88, 98,149, 166, 174, 175

Shutterstock p21, 55, 67, 81, 99, 107, 167, 171

Unknown Source p84

Historical Mapping Credit:

Reproduced with the permission of the National Library of Scotland

To view the full licence terms, visit:
https://creativecommons.org/licenses/by/4.0/

ACKNOWLEDGEMENTS

Thank you to the many people who have worked hard to make this book happen, including: Nick Giles, Kris Mackenzie, Mark Wolstenholme, Paul McGonigal, Bel Dixon, Sam Emberson, Liz Beverley, Helen Newman, Sam Lovell, Nicoletta Cremona, Jo Lines, Stephen Hartwell, Gavin Cliffe, Mike Johnson, Katie Hopkins, Mandy Brereton, Richard Harper, Alice Cunningham, Carolyne Lawton, Rhea Pinfield, Peter Reynolds, Harry O'Reilly, Andy Steggall, Camilla Dowson, David Jones, the OS Consumer Team, the OS Cartographic Team, Iwan Thomas and Adam Gauntlett.

Ordnance Survey

Fancy brushing up on your navigational skills and solving even more fiendish puzzles?

Why not get yourself copies of *The Ordnance Survey Puzzle Book*, *The Ordnance Survey Puzzle Tour of Britain*, *The Ordnance Survey Great British Treasure Hunt* and *The Ordnance Survey Journey Through Time*, and pit your wits against Britain's greatest map makers?

Share your adventures and puzzle-solving with us:

 os.uk/blog   @ordnancesurvey

 @OSLeisure   @osmapping